MW00736980

CONTRARY
CREEK

PEOPLE AND THEIR HORSES

HOOFBEATS

ACROSS

AMERICA

BY THE AUTHORS AT CONTRARY CREEK

Lucile Davis
Renee Prindle Jones
Rachel Stowe Master
Don Patterson
Dr. Punch Shaw
Terry Wilson

Allison Fisher
Fran Lowe
Will McDonald
C.C. Risenhoover
Diane Stafford

CONTRARY
CREEK

Copyright © 2001 by Georgia Risenhoover

All rights reserved. No part of this book may be reproduced in any form or by any electronic or mechanical means, including information storage and retrieval systems, without permission in writing from the publisher, except by a reviewer, who may quote brief passages in a review.

Printed in the United States of America

FIRST EDITION

Library of Congress Cataloging-in-Publication Data

Risenhoover, Georgia
        Hoof Beats Across America / Georgia Risenhoover. – 1st ed.
        p. cm.
        ISBN 0-9677291-2-2
        LCCN 2001089662

DESIGN BY JEFF STANTON

Published by Contrary Creek Publishers

FOR
AMERICA'S
HORSE
LOVERS

THE LEGACY LIVES ON

In the fall of 1999, life was pleasant and normal for the close-knit Albright family. Harold and his wife Judy lived on a 500-acre ranch deep within the scenic pine forests of Willis, Texas, about 60 miles north of Houston. Their three sons, Wade, Kevin and Kyle, helped Harold on a regular basis with his small business in the city. The family enjoyed traveling together on weekends to various horse shows, so the boys could compete in challenging cutting horse events.

On October 13 of that year, the Albrights experienced a major tragedy that changed their lives forever. Without any previous warning, Harold, in his 50s, died of a heart attack, leaving his wife and sons with the heartrending grief that goes along with such a catastrophe.

"Many people have to face sudden death situations, but this was

< 3 >

a real shock to me," Judy said. "I cope as well as I can, but it's hard to readjust after 35 years of marriage."

Yet Judy, a born-again Christian, said she realizes that she will see Harold again in heaven when she passes away.

The close-knit bond that developed in the family has become even stronger after Harold's passing. Kevin, a bachelor born in 1973, has stayed with his mother at the ranch to help her out with all the daily chores, including mowing with the tractor, taking care of the colts and mares and working the cattle. His twin, Kyle, and brother, Wade (2 years older), who have families of their own, drive up every other weekend from their suburban homes in Pearland to give him a hand with training the young horses and working the cattle.

JUDY SAID HER SONS NEVER WENT THROUGH THE DREADED TEENAGE REBELLION YEARS.

Kevin enjoys working with the animals on the ranch and being outdoors.

"I like being out in the country, away from city life," he said.

Since he was a senior in high school, he has raised pedigree Limousin cattle, but prefers his show horses to cows. At 13, he started showing cutting horses at the Houston Livestock Show and Rodeo and at similar events throughout Texas. His favorite show was the 1991 Chevy Truck Final 10,000 Non-Pro in Jackson, Mississippi, where he won a gold cutting horse necklace for his mother.

Not to be outdone by their brother, Kyle and Wade also performed well in cutting horse competitions during their teens and early 20s. Kyle showed his favorite mare, Conticha Gay Rebel, in the non-pro class at the Houston show and won $120,000. In his senior year of high school, Wade was the reserve champion at the 1989 NCHA Summer Spectacular Derby in Fort Worth, aboard Bingo Hickory.

"The boys rooted for each other all the time," Judy said. "There was never any bickering among them, because they all worked together."

Judy said that because of the closeness of the family, her sons never went through the dreaded teenage rebellion years that have plagued so many families. Harold was their Little League coach and she was the team mom and "room mother."

"We have always tried to support the boys and be involved in

< 4 >

their lives," she said. "As a result, we never had any problems with them. Their dad always had the last word. Whatever he said, that's what they would do."

Like his sons, Harold enjoyed horses at a young age and often went to rodeos to participate in the calf-roping events. His brother, Jack, told Judy that during one competition, he literally "charmed" one of the calves. After Harold had roped the calf and jumped off his horse, he ran up to him.

"The calf lay perfectly still, put his four legs together, and Harold finished tying the legs together, winning the event," Judy said, chuckling.

Because of his rodeo experience in his youth, Harold loved chatting and kidding with the cowboys competing in the shows.

"They all wanted to know how he knew how to be a cowboy, because they didn't know he had rodeoed," Judy said. "He told a boy one time, 'I have more backup time on a horse than you have going forward.'"

After that conversation, Harold decided that he would show for a year to see what he could accomplish. He had the good fortune and skill it takes to ride a cutting horse to place in the top ten in the world of the 10,000 Non-Pro NCHA class in 1991. He received his belt buckle in the cutting horse arena at the Houston Livestock Show and Rodeo, much to the amazement of everyone. Judy said that Harold's fellow participants had been trying to win for years.

> "HE NEVER HAD TROUBLE WITH ANYONE ASKING HIM WHAT HE COULD DO ANYMORE."

"He never had trouble with anyone asking him what he could do anymore," she said.

Then, Harold set his sights on showing his 6-year-old prize stud stallion, Bingo, for the first time at an NCHA Abilene spectacular event. All the trainers came back to watch him, because "they didn't think this 'fat boy' could show", Judy said.

Again, Harold surprised everyone, even his sons, by winning the cutting horse event.

"My brothers and I had been showing for five years," Wade said with admiration. "Here comes Dad who goes on to win the whole competition."

<5>

Judy said Harold also had great success selecting and buying quality horses. Bingo, a son of champions Doc's Hickory and Bingo Quixote, won more money than any cutting horse in 1988. In 2000, his colts had already won more than $670,000 in area competitions.

"Harold knew the pedigree on the horse, and he was so super excited when he had the opportunity to buy him that he could hardly contain himself," she said.

Judy admitted that she enjoyed taking care of the horses, but it was Harold who loved to talk about them. He had always dreamed about owning a ranch, so when he had the opportunity to purchase the beautiful 500-acre spread in Willis, he jumped on it.

"He made it a complete success," Judy said. "It was his baby, and he rocked it."

When Harold and Judy got married in 1963, he was working on the docks of the Houston Ship Channel. Judy said he was itching to do something different, so in 1980 started his own oil valve business with a $2,000 income tax refund check. Harold had figured out that no one else had cornered the market on forged steel valves, so he decided to fill the need with his unique company. Judy said that Harold taught himself about valves, and never went anywhere without a valve book in his hand.

> "HE MADE IT A COMPLETE SUCCESS," JUDY SAID. "IT WAS HIS BABY, AND HE ROCKED IT."

"He was a self-made man," she said. "I was so proud of him for making the business such a success."

His three sons regularly assisted him with the sales and distribution for the prosperous business. After Harold died, however, they found themselves running the whole operation. For Wade, the new president and CEO, his new position gave him a completely new perspective about his father.

"I realize now what Dad had to handle every day," Wade said. "I didn't know what running a business was like until I was put into the position."

Even though the brothers take the business seriously, they give themselves time for relaxation. They do not compete in the rodeo arena much anymore because of the time it requires to prepare the horses, so they have turned their attention to golf and hunting. Wade and Kyle

< 6 >

enjoy the competitive aspect of golf so much that they often play in tournaments at the Woodlands, Lake Conroe, Bentwater and Golfcrest Country Club in Pearland. Harold had also liked golf, and he made some excellent friends with golfers at those courses. In fact, they served as pallbearers at his funeral.

Wade sees both similarities and differences between golf matches and cutting horse events.

"Both sports require a great deal of focus," Wade said. "Golf, however, takes six hours to play, and riding a cutting horse in the arena takes only two and a half minutes. Another difference is that when I'm riding cutting horses in the show arena, there's no room for mistakes. In golf, you can get it right on the next hole."

The brothers still love horses and hope to pass on the legacy that their father left them to their own children. In a few years, Kyle wants to get his son, Payton (born in 1998), involved with horses.

> "HORSES ALWAYS KEPT US OCCUPIED, AND HELPED TO HOLD OUR FAMILY TOGETHER."

"Dad put us on to horses, and it kept us out of a lot of stuff going on in the city," he said. "Horses always kept us occupied, and helped to hold our family together. I want my son to have the same experience."

< 7 >

JEFF
KIRKBRIDE
Photography

HARD KNOCKS

ancher Bud Alderson reminds you of the words to that James Taylor song. You know, the one about seeing fire and rain and sunny days he thought would never end.

Born in 1922, Alderson has seen all of that and more. Much, much more.

And these days, almost as active as ever, the only real problem with Bud Alderson is getting him out of the barn long enough to talk to him. He loves to putter around out there. And besides, he still has horses to feed and tend and train. So if you get the idea he's a no-non-sense cowboy, you're right – but he does have a good sense of humor.

"I started out in 1948," he said in reference to his long stint as a professional quarter horse judge, "and I quit in 1995. Myself, I didn't

< 9 >

get to go to college, but I learned my lessons at home and through hard knocks."

Following rules to the letter was an important part of Alderson's integrity. And, basically, he chose to bow out of judging while he was still on a high note.

FOLLOWING RULES TO THE LETTER WAS AN IMPORTANT PART OF ALDERSON'S INTEGRITY.

"After so long a time, I see some of these professional judges today even, when they get to the place where they don't follow rules," he said. "There are so many things you have to remember."

Alderson said one day he stepped in the ring to judge, "And I couldn't think of anything. I had too much ego to talk about what was happening. So I went down to the arena, and when the first horse came in, all of a sudden, I knew it all again."

But the moment unnerved him.

"I had been doing it long enough," he said. "They take you off the quarter horse judging list automatically when you're 70, and I was past that."

He said he wanted to go out while he was still in demand – and he did.

"We had done well going all over the country," Alderson said. "I'd been telling myself I needed to quit while I was ahead."

At Alderson Quarter Horse Farm, the children, Randy and Janelle, got their share of horse exposure while growing up. As a result Randy is a horse judge himself, and his daughter, Andrea, born in 1983, shows horses. He also has a son, Aaron, born in 1988.

Alderson's other grandchildren are Janelle's kids – Brian, born 1980, and Katie, born 1983.

The day he came out of the barn to do some talking was in the summer of 2000 and his granddaughter was in Fort Worth, Texas entered in the world quarter horse youth finals.

"It's the third year she has gone to finals," he said. "She's already placed good, but this class is tough. She shows good horses we raised."

Pointing proudly to the headline that described him in a horse-journal article as "Bud Alderson: A judge of character," he said, "For 25 years I was on the rules committee."

Featured widely in horse journals, Alderson judged horses in 48

< 1 0 >

states and many foreign countries. Today, he is on the amateur committee.

"And I'm an honorary vice-president of the American Quarter Horse Association," he said.

In fact, one of his favorite outings is the annual quarter horse convention.

"I get to see people I met from years back," he said. "In 2001, I'll get a plaque for raising quarter horse colts for 50 years in a row."

Judging horses is no simple matter.

"There's so many things horses are judged on," Alderson said. "The Quarter Horse is a breed association, and that covers all kinds of horses, from reining to cutting to racing to pleasure to conformation...all kinds. So, you have to make a decision on what you want to raise.

"In 1960 I went on as a national director for the Quarter Horse Association. I was the only one Indiana had for years."

Now he raises pleasure horses "because there's more demand for them."

"I've done a little bit of both...riding and raising," he said. "In 1978 in quarter horse competition, I had high point all-around at the Quarter Horse Congress with Lad's Imperial, and he's one of only two studs who have been high point all-around."

JUDGING HORSES IS NO SIMPLE MATTER.

His memorabilia from long years of horsemanship is sparse because of a barn fire on January 18, 1994 that burned up horse, records and trophies.

"It was 27 below zero that night, and we never found out what happened," he said. "We think it was an electrical fire. We had two stallions at that time—one was a former world champion—and they both burned up. I had many championship trophies."

He shudders at the memory of that awful chapter in his life.

"This was devastating to us," he said. "I wanted to quit. I told my wife we could take insurance money, and we could just go some place. And she said, 'I don't know where you'd go...you've been everywhere.'"

Speaking of the horses he lost, he said, "I was not only fond of them but they were valuable. But we've done well since, so that's good.

<11>

"I grew up with parents that were farmers; we did all of our work farming with horses. I grew up knowing about draft horses. At age 10, I worked draft horses."

That did not, however, make him a horse lover.

"No," he said, "it was hard work. The only playing time you ever had was on Sunday, and then there wasn't much to do. When I was 6 years old, at a county fair, I even raced a pony my dad had got for me. I got to do some things kids today don't get to do.

"Every day I go out into the barn to check on the horses. We have 40 horses around here. We have full-time hired help, but it's a habit going out there to take care of and train the horses. In the fall we show at a lot of the futurities, so I enjoy getting the babies and yearlings ready for that."

A practical man, Alderson claims he does not fall in love with his animals.

"I like the ones that can do the most for me," he said.

But he then goes on to tell of one of his first standouts—Toledo, a King-Ranch-bred horse born in 1960.

"He was a great horse for me," he said, "and then we lucked onto Lad's Imperial, a Skipper W-bred stallion, at this congress."

Do horses have personalities?

"Oh, my, yes," he said. "These two had great personalities and a lot of ability. I like ones with a good attitude."

After sharing his life with these mighty beasts, Bud Alderson has no fear of them.

"I feel like I'm as big as they are," he said. "I can read their minds because I've done this all my life."

> "I GREW UP WITH PARENTS THAT WERE FARMERS; WE DID ALL OF OUR WORK FARMING WITH HORSES."

Although Alderson won't admit to any sentimentality, he thinks his wife, Madonna, is definitely prone to be that way.

"She's sentimental about her mare, oh, yeah," he said. "She gets attached to her horses and doesn't like to sell them. Her mare, Zip's Gold Lassie, was high-point pleasure horse in the nation in 1993, and now is a brood mare."

BUD ALDERSON

When Alderson judged, he got a reputation for being a judge who was tough, with high standards, but who was fair.

"You got to be decent yourself, for somebody to like you," he said. "I think people always believed what I said."

Sometimes, it distressed him that some people could become so obsessed with winning that it led to drugs and "doctored tails."

He said, "Some people would do this doctoring – they would deaden the tail up around the root where it comes out of the body, to keep them from switching the tail...because in competition, switching the tail isn't good. You can also breed them not to do it."

Horse shows have politics, he said, "just like in everything else. But I was never political...I did my own thing whether they liked it or not."

The white-haired horseman still wears a Silver Belly-colored cowboy hat.

> HORSE SHOWS HAVE POLITICS, HE SAID, "JUST LIKE IN EVERYTHING ELSE."

"But you know what?" he said, laughing. "My hair used to be black. Something happened. But I've got most my hair...and I'm glad about that.

"I wear Levi's year-round, especially out farming. I love them and they're pretty tough, and today I like an ostrich boot. They wear real good. My boots are soft, and they feel good. You can't get them for less than $400, and when I was a kid, you could get a pair of boots for $20."

In 1949, Alderson said he owned the first quarter horse stallion ever to stand grand champion east of the Mississippi at the Indiana State Fair.

Asked if it was one of his most cherished moments, he replied, "Boy, yes. That was the first quarter horse show ever held east of the Mississippi. The quarter horse started in 1940, and then it was just around Texas and Oklahoma. That horse was a yearling and his daddy was a horse I raced for a man...Tiger Joe Bailey. I didn't have 15 cents, and he let me breed my mare for nothing. I didn't realize at the time what I'd really done, and luckily, I still have both of these trophies, one for winning the class and the other for grand champion."

How much does a good quarter horse cost today?

< 13 >

"It's so variable it's unreal," Alderson said, adding that it can be anywhere from $2,500 to $4 million.

"We've never seen the monetary situation like it is today," he said. "A lot [of horses] will sell up in the millions. In our case, we've bought horses we could afford, and we've been fortunate to make them into something."

> "I ENJOYED JUDGING ALL OVER THE U.S. AND IN THE FOREIGN COUNTRIES."

He called selling horses "a breed situation" and said, "Some we sell for good money and some not, but they have to get a new home. That's our business.

"I enjoyed judging all over the U.S. and in the foreign countries. My dad told me you've got to work, and it won't come easy. I farmed 700 acres besides and I raised 1,000 head of hogs a year, from little baby pigs until I'd feed them out when they weighed 220 pounds. So you kept them around quite a while. I'm talking about work. And they smell bad."

Who is Bud Alderson today?

He laughed at the question and replied, "Basically, I'm a has-been, but I've had some good moments. I always thought that I worked for them. Only thing, it bothers me greatly that I can't do what I did five or six years ago. Used to, I'd run a foot race from the barn to the road and beat anybody, but not anymore.

"Over the years, I've had so many friends. I've picked up so much, with so many people so good to me."

He told of feeling angry and aggravated a few years ago when he saw eight pages of magazine advertising bought by a horse breeder.

"He was a very rich guy from the East," he said. "My thought was, you couldn't get a placing from me (as a judge) with an ad in the paper. They had to earn everything they got in front of me."

But Alderson admitted that he had the guy pegged wrong.

"He came up to me at a show in Florida, and invited my wife and me to stay in his guest house," Alderson said. "He told me he appreciated everything I'd done. He wanted to raise horses, and he was proud when he got a placement from me. He didn't want to be given any gifts."

< 14 >

BUD ALDERSON

Bud Alderson is a cowboy with high principles and a tough-on-himself attitude. The way other folks see it, no one makes a better horse judge. A placing from him really means something. He can't be bought, and he won't cut you any slack; he knows horses, and he knows good ones when he sees them.

"My wife gets mad at me because I'm a critic of our own stock," he said, "but I've judged so many years, I know what good ones are. So, I always think ours are not as good as they should be."

Alderson said the horse business has been a good thing for him.

"Anybody who has ever been around horses knows that it does something for you," he said, "whether or not you're good at it. It's been fun, and the fact that you can handle that big animal is good for you. And I've handled a few thousand over the years."

<15>

CALVIN & BRENDA ALLEN

CRAFTING TRADITION

alvin Allen knows about tradition. A saddle maker, he continues the tradition of cutting, shaping and stitching high quality saddles from the finest materials available.

After learning the craft in Fort Worth, Texas saddle shops, Allen branched out on his own and founded his own saddlery in Weatherford, Texas, about 20 miles west of Fort Worth.

"The secret to saddle-making is always knowing what you are going to do next," said Allen, pointing out the extensive amount of stitching holding one of his saddles together.

He said shaping the leather properly requires carefully wetting the leather so that the proper shape can be attained at the precise moment that it needs to be stitched. And there's a lot of shaping and stitching

< 17 >

involved. It takes about 35 hours of labor for him to cut, shape and hand-stitch the leather to make just one of his cutting horse saddles.

But Allen doesn't mind. Clearly, he takes great pride in his work and reputation. He wants it done right.

Raised in Virginia, Allen moved to Weatherford to attend Weatherford College. After college he moved to Stephenville, Texas, then to the nearby town of Dublin where he married his wife, Brenda. Eventually they moved back to Weatherford so that they could be closer to Fort Worth, the cutting horse capital of the world, yet still enjoy the pleasures of rural life.

HE TAKES GREAT PRIDE IN HIS WORK AND REPUTATION. HE WANTS IT DONE RIGHT.

After the couple settled in Weatherford, they opened their saddlery business.

With 25 years of saddle making experience, Calvin produces his own line of cutting horse saddles and tack. The saddle shop also sells a wide variety of apparel and supplies to equip local horse people.

Brenda spends most of her time handling the business affairs of the shop, building relationships with customers and managing the books. The two sell their wares through their family-owned store in Weatherford and take their store on the road to various horse shows throughout the year.

But the Allens don't spend all of their time working with leather and running the business. They also continue the tradition of fine horsemanship during their off-hours.

Brenda has had quite a bit of success in the arena. A champion barrel racer, she has gradually made the transition to cutting horse competitions over the last few years. The specialized skills required for cutting horse competition appeal to Brenda.

"I like the competition," she said. "I love to ride, but I like to have a purpose."

Brenda has had some great horses over the years. One of her favorites was Miss Copbaretta. Obtained from Martha Josey, Miss Copbaretta was a fast, athletic chestnut sorrel with a flax mane and tail.

"She had a big heart and lots of try," said Brenda.

Another of Brenda's favorites was A Sharp Contender, a short sorrel gelding. Brenda won over $250,000 in 14 years of competition with

< 18 >

CALVIN & BRENDA ALLEN

A Sharp Contender.

This interest in cutting horses has translated itself to their business. The Calvin Allen Saddlery specializes in cutting horse saddles. Terry Riddle, Bill Freeman and Buster Welch, all National Cutting Horse Hall of Fame Riders, heavily influenced the Calvin Allen designs.

But seeing Brenda managing the Calvin Allen Saddlery booth at shows reveals that there is more to her love of cutting horse competitions than simply riding and competing. She clearly enjoys the people she meets and the camaraderie and friendly competition of the cutting horse set.

Although Calvin doesn't participate in as many competitions as Brenda does, he is something of an amateur historian. But he doesn't just read about history, he makes it come alive – on horseback.

Calvin participates in reenactments of 19th century cavalry regiments in full period costumes and with equipment from the period. In the company of men with a similar interest, he rehearses cavalry tactics and participates in some of the larger Civil War reenactments.

The saddle maker also participates in the annual Weatherford reenactments that are sponsored by the Weatherford Chamber of Commerce. The Weatherford event has a special day for school children to come to the site and witness the living history on display. These special days help local children understand history and get a sense of what it must have been like to be a cavalry soldier well over 100 years ago.

Calvin is also a member of the Texas Division of the Sons of Confederate Veterans, a group dedicated to preserving the history and heritage of the Southern cause during the Civil War. The SCV fights any attempt to tarnish or distort the image of the Confederate soldier and his reasons for fighting. SCV members focus on education and work with schools and youth organizations to provide an understanding of the reasons and causes for the secession of the Southern states.

> HE DOESN'T JUST READ ABOUT HISTORY, HE MAKES IT COME ALIVE – ON HORSEBACK.

The Allens are proud of their heritage. Whether it is the tradition of saddle making, working cattle with a cutting horse or preserving the heritage and history of Southern life, Calvin and Brenda Allen live their traditions and past them on to future generations.

<19>

LONG RIDE THROUGH MEMORIES

Earle V. (Buddy) Almy's horse memories go back to a time and place where folks didn't saddle up just for fun – they did it to get from one place to another.

"My sister and I used to ride our horses to school every day," said Buddy, a real estate appraiser in Granbury, Texas. "We used to tie them up on a vacant lot right there on Stadium Drive across from Alice E. Carlson Elementary School in Fort Worth."

Ironically, the site of Buddy's hitching post is now home to the School of Ranch Management at Texas Christian University.

"Of course, my sister and I didn't just ride to school," he said, chuckling. "We used to race each other. She had a pony named Snowball, but I won most of the races on my horse, Tony. She got

< 21 >

upset over that and told Dad she wanted a faster horse. So he got her a little thin, fast, paint horse named Queenie, and soon she was leaving me and Tony in a cloud of dust."

However, despite his efforts to get to school quickly, Buddy was not always welcome once he got there.

"I used to run my trap line every morning," said Buddy, alluding to his days as a fur trapper. "And I'd trap all sorts of things – possum, skunks and even a mink, a fox and a raccoon. Others in the classroom often noticed that I smelled like a skunk."

> "OTHERS IN THE CLASSROOM OFTEN NOTICED THAT I SMELLED LIKE A SKUNK."

Buddy's view of life from the practical side of a horse continued through his high school years when he worked a summer for the famed Reynolds Ranch in Kent, Texas.

"It was a mighty big ranch," Buddy said. "It was 300 sections in size. We would wear a horse out in the morning and have to get a new one in the afternoon.

"We had bulls that wanted to fight one another and cows that were crazy from eating loco weed. They were frothing at the mouth and going after anything that got in their way. It was hard to work them because those bulls would try to kill a horse and the horses knew it."

For Buddy such problems were minor compared to the difficulty of keeping seven horses shod – another chore the cowboys were supposed to take care of themselves.

"I still have an enormous amount of respect for anybody who can shoe a horse," he said, readily admitting it was what he liked least about ranch work.

"We would also help round up cattle and do cutting for the Edwards ranch that was nearby. And ranch work was no easier than today, but it was more adventurous."

Buddy's next career move should have continued to keep him on horseback, but somehow it did not work out that way. He enrolled at Texas Tech University and earned a degree in animal husbandry – something that seemed sure to keep him involved in horses and livestock.

< 2 2 >

Moreover, it did.

During college, he worked for the Mill Iron Ranch in Estelline, Texas. Besides rounding up cattle everyday, he kept five horses shod on the 200-section ranch.

In an era when the draft threatened two years in the Army for any young man, Buddy chose four years in the Air Force. Unfortunately the Air Force had no horses, but his animal husbandry degree was put to good use by making him a "veterinary technician," an unusual title in the Air Force.

"I wound up inspecting shrimp in Brownsville, Texas," said Buddy, who to this day sounds a little surprised by what happened to him. "I inspected over a million pounds of shrimp, which went to the officer's clubs throughout the world, everywhere we had troops. We inspected all of the food that came onto the base before it was eaten by the troops."

After the military, life continued to conspire to keep Buddy in the livestock field but away from horses. However, his first job after discharge was as a repo man for a bank.

"I did that for about three years," he said, "then finally went and told my boss, 'You need to take me off this. I'm developing a complex. Everybody I see looks like a deadbeat to me.'"

After a few more years with the bank, working in the loan and discount department as well as the financial analysis department, Buddy got closer to his agricultural roots by taking a job in Saginaw, Texas.

> "I TOLD MY BOSS 'I DON'T GIVE A DAMN ABOUT THESE CHICKENS.'"

After a short time, he became director of finance and poultry feed sales for Burrus Feed Mill for 14 territories in five states. It was not, however, a promotion he particularly relished.

"I told my boss my degree was in animal husbandry, not poultry husbandry and that 'I don't give a damn about these chickens.' And my boss said, 'Well you can learn.'"

Buddy subsequently traveled to Iowa to be trained to inspect chickens and other poultry for disease – a practice called "posting." When he found sick birds, he had to post them. He said that when he

< 23 >

visited his salesmen in their far-flung rural territories, they would greet him with "Here comes Dr. Almy."

"I'm not a veterinarian and never wanted to be a veterinarian," said Buddy. "But they would say, 'take a look at my sick turkeys' or 'my chickens are sick' and I would have to go over and post them. I had about a year of that and was fed up with it. I asked my boss for some other job, so he gave me the Fort Worth territory to work."

Buddy eventually found his true calling when he returned to selling farms and ranches, something he had done in his years in the banking industry. In February 1970 he opened Almy and Company Realtors in Hurst, Texas, and moved to Granbury, Texas in 1979. He earned his state certified general real estate appraiser designation in 1992.

"I have been selling and appraising property since 1959, which hasn't left much room for horses," Buddy said. "Wish to heck I had one."

However, he has been able to keep riding. He rides a horse over some of the ranches before he sells them.

"I LOVE GOD'S WORK IN NATURE AND I LOVE HORSES"

Although the demands of his business have prevented him from riding on a regular basis, Buddy (born in 1930) is an avid fan of cutting horse competitions and is even a member of the National Cutting Horse Association. Buddy also spends time at Lone Star Park in Grand Prairie, Texas, watching the Thoroughbreds and Quarter Horses race.

"My true desire all of my life is to have my own ranch. I love God's work in nature and I love horses, especially a well-groomed black stallion, better than anything else."

< 2 4 >

MEL BLOUNT

HEART OF A CHAMPION

Webster's defines a "champion" as "one that is acknowledged to be better than all others" or as "a militant advocate or defender."

Mel Blount definitely fits into both categories – on and off the football field.

During the glory days of the Pittsburgh Steelers in the '70s, Blount was famous for his aggressive defensive play as a cornerback. In 1975 he led the National Football League in interceptions with 11 and was named the NFL's defensive Most Valuable Player (MVP).

Blount had 57 career interceptions for 736 yards, more than any player in Steeler history; played in five Pro Bowls; six American Football Conference (AFC) Championships; and in Super Bowls IX, X, XIII and XIV (all won by Pittsburgh).

< 27 >

After retiring in 1983, he was enshrined in the Pro Football Hall of Fame during his first year of eligibility, and was later inducted into the State Hall of Fame in both Louisiana and Georgia in 1990.

When the Steelers drafted Blount out of Southern University in Louisiana in 1970, he used his bonus money to buy three horses. After he was in the pros for a while, he enjoyed his new hobby so much that he ended up buying more cutting horses. He soon discovered that riding horses was a good way for him to get out and relax during the off-season.

"I COULD GO HOME AND UNWIND BY RIDING MY HORSE."

"I give horses a lot of credit for my success, because I knew I always had an outlet when the pressure got to be too much," Blount said. "I would look forward to the off-season when I could go home and unwind by riding my horse. I never got a chance to ride horses during the season because there was so much demand on my time."

Blount said he has always liked horses, since his early years growing up as one of 11 children on the family farm in Vidalia, Georgia. His parents grew soybeans, cotton and corn. And, of course, they used horses and mules to do plowing and other work around the farm.

One horse in particular, Tony, was used for everything from plowing to hauling wagons and pulling sleds.

"Tony was like part of the family," Blount recalled. "Back in those days we cooked on wood-burning stoves, and we would open up the kitchen window. He would come to the window, and we would feed him some bread or corn."

When Blount was a sophomore in college, Tony died, and Blount admits to having "cried like a baby."

His six brothers assured him that his family would get another horse. They bought a mare named Maud, who produced a colt that they raised.

After Blount retired from football he bought a farm in Claysville, Pennsylvania, along with some cutting horses that had excellent bloodlines. He now trains and shows horses with the same competitive drive that he exhibited on the playing field.

In 1999, he won a split fourth with Paula Woods in the futurity

< 2 8 >

MEL BLOUNT

event at the National Cutting Horse Association (NCHA) World Championship.

"I have a great appreciation for good athletes," Blount said. "I don't care if they're barrel horses, or reining horses or pleasure horses, but my love and passion is cutting horses."

Blount admitted that when he first showed a horse, he looked like a greenhorn. He said Bud Webb, the NCHA member he bought the horse from, told him to "give her as much slack as you can and let her do the work."

Blount said he complied, but the reins were so long the horse almost stepped on them. Renowned cutting horse breeder Norman Bruce took Blount aside and told him that he could teach him the sport. It was eight years later before he could make it out to Bruce's farm, but once he got there, the cutting horse breeder taught him what he needed to know.

In training his own horses on his farm, the former football great feels that he has developed a special bond with them.

"I can relate to them from being an athlete and having to work hard in training," Blount said. "I know that when I was in football, I didn't want someone messing with me all the time. Instead, I wanted my coach to show me what to do, and then leave me alone. I treat my horses the same way. I know when a horse is trying to give me his best and when he's not. Even though they can't talk to me, I watch the way they act and know when they're feeling good or bad. Sports has been a great training ground for me to move into raising horses, and I really have an appreciation, and a special kind of understanding of what they go through."

> "MY LOVE AND PASSION IS CUTTING HORSES."

Blount said he also enjoys his large blended family; his wife, Tianda, two adult daughters and three young sons. His children love horses, too, and often ride around the ranch with their father. The youngest, born in 1996, rides by himself inside a small round pen, and Blount said the horse good-naturedly lets him "crawl all over his back."

Besides being a champion on the football field and in the horse arena, Blount is also a hero in the eyes of some troubled young boys who have looked to him for encouragement, support and even shelter.

<29>

He said he has seen too many of them that are lost in a system that is failing them.

Shortly after he retired from football in 1983, Blount founded a youth home on a farm in his hometown of Vidalia, Georgia, to assist young boys in their pursuit to become productive members of society. Longing to do even more, in 1989 he decided to establish another youth home near his adopted hometown of Pittsburgh.

After some trying times and many hours of hard work, he succeeded in building a youth home in a rural location near Claysville, Pennsylvania. In his book, *The Cross Burns Brightly*, Blount tells all about the trials and tribulations that he went through to establish the youth homes.

Blount's compassion, service and perseverance have already given many young men the opportunity and the desire to pursue their potential. In fact, a large part of Blount's treatment program allows the young boys to work with his horses. They help him break the colts using a patient and gentle style that emphasizes safety first.

"MANY OF THEM THAT ARE LOST IN A SYSTEM THAT IS FAILING THEM."

"These kids who grew up in the inner city have a lot of respect and love for horses, maybe because they're big," Blount said. "These kids are supposed to be so tough, but whenever they run up against something they don't know about, there's a certain amount of fear. But once they discover that the horses are gentle, loving and easy to be around, they develop a love for them. The first thing the kids say who have been through our program is how much they miss the horses."

Blount usually houses a total of 70 white and African-American boys in the two homes. His vision is to found more youth homes throughout the United States. In the future he also wants to take the boys to show the horses at the Youth World competition.

For Blount, the youth homes have been both frustrating and rewarding experiences.

"It's been a real roller coaster ride, because it's tough working with troubled kids who have come from dysfunctional families, but overall it's been a wonderful as well as challenging experience."

< 3 1 >

NOT JUST FOR THE KIDS

Good parents are always thinking about ways to enrich the lives of their children. They strive to make them happy and want them to enjoy growing up in a healthy family environment. They particularly want to share with their offspring, the joys they experienced while they were growing up. Good parents try to select the best experiences from their youth and recreate them for their own children.

Jim and Sandi Blumer are not exceptions from that parental role. They wanted their youngsters to enjoy the fun of riding horses, just as they had during their youth. They wanted them to also appreciate the beauty and grace of the equine species.

"I had always been around horses," Jim said. "I was raised on a small 20 acre farm and we always had a few horses. My grandfather

< 3 3 >

raised show horses and entered them in American Quarter Horse Association (AQHA) competitions. I can't remember a time when we didn't have a horse."

So Jim and Sandi Blumer decided to breed a few horses for the benefit of their children. They rightly believed that showing their kids how to ride and care for the horses would teach them greater values.

JIM AND SANDI DECIDED TO BREED A FEW HORSES FOR THE BENEFIT OF THEIR CHILDREN.

Little did they realize, however, that in buying a few horses, they would become involved in a great adventure. For in just a few short years, Jim and Sandi would undergo a dramatic career change, enter a fiercely competitive business and ultimately discover the fulfillment of their lifelong dreams in a venture that paid great monetary and spiritual rewards.

The Blumers' original career field had been in the health care arena. Jim had wanted to become an accountant, but found a challenge in developing and managing health care facilities. Sandi was a professional nurse, so had the medical background to support Jim in the venture.

Jim and Sandi soon found themselves operating eleven nursing homes and assisted living facilities in northeastern Pennsylvania where they lived. They led a staff of 350 employees and although successful in their vocation, found it stressful and demanding. When the lure of horse breeding suddenly loomed on the horizon, they welcomed its coming.

This new enterprise came unexpectedly and somewhat by chance. While Jim was shopping for horses for the children, he learned that Willowbrook Farms, a well-respected horse breeding operation in the Allentown area, was going out of the horse-breeding business.

Jim negotiated from Willowbrook, the sale of five excellent brood mares with foals at their sides. Jim entertained prospects of earning back his investment through their offspring.

The deal would, indeed, serve to earn much more. The purchase would first introduce the children to the adventure of caring for newborn horses. Sandi, who already loved horses, was pleased at the under-

< 3 4 >

taking and looked forward to nursing the mares through their pregnancies. Moreover, the purchase became a ticket to a whole new business excursion for the Blumers.

Within a year the couple owned 15 horses, both having been severely bitten by the horse-breeding bug.

In the coming months Jim and Sandi continued their originally unplanned excursion into the horse breeding profession. They learned by doing, but not without research and careful planning. They studied other successful breeders and sought advice from established owners, trainers and horsemen.

Although Jim hadn't ridden professionally, he visited local horse shows, then traveled to other shows about the country to learn more about show horse competitions. Ultimately, Jim entered riding competitions with his well-trained horses and was soon on the way to winning several major championships throughout the nation.

Jim's prize stallion, Lenas Sugarman has won numerous awards in National Cutting Horse Association (NCHA), American Cutting Horse Association (ACHA), and National Reining Horse Association (NRHA) championships. The stallion has sired more than 60 AQHA registered foals including prize-winning stallions and award-winning mares.

Jim can't say enough about his multi-prize-winner.

"In September of 1999, Sugarman won two Morrison and a Lawson bronze in NRHA Open World Competition," Jim said, proudly. "He is now (2000) currently third in open world standings. I have to give special thanks to his trainer, Rocky Dare.

"Another of our horses, Play For Chic was eighth at NCHA Open Futurity, in December 1999, earning over $46,000. I give special thanks to trainer Kathy Daughn, who did an outstanding job. In April 2000, Play for Chic took fourth place in Open 2000 Super Stakes."

"Sugarman," Jim continued, "qualified for the Semifinals in the USET reining at Oklahoma City. But that," said Jim, "is only the beginning."

> THEY LEARNED BY DOING, BUT NOT WITHOUT RESEARCH AND CAREFUL PLANNING.

< 3 5 >

Beginning operation in 1992, the Blumer's Double J Quarter Horses enterprise in Moscow, Pennsylvania is flourishing and growing. Blumer uses a familiar eastern Pennsylvania expression to describe their progress.

"We are moving forward, 'nine-oh' or full speed ahead to build our ranch into an even greater facility," Jim said. "We are installing a large outdoor track, expanding our breeding-capacity and capabilities, and modernizing our methods. Add to that, the everyday routine activities of cleaning stalls, feeding, exercising and breeding mares, and you've got a full time operation. Fortunately we have an excellent staff of trainers and hands. They work together to make our operation shine. Our goal is to breed the best horses we can and to fully trust the bloodline. I'm confident we are going to achieve and maintain that objective."

The intense nature of the horse business has not caused the Blumers to neglect their children. Whitney (born 1987), James (born 1989) and Jenna (born 1992) all share in the successful venture.

"All the kids are interested in what we do, but our youngest is the bravest," Jim said. "Yet, we aren't directing the kids to follow our lead in horse-breeding, training or riding. Sandi and I want them to choose their own directions in life. We let them learn and discover at their own pace. Our youngest, however, is showing considerable interest."

> THE INTENSE NATURE OF THE HORSE BUSINESS HAS NOT CAUSED THE BLUMERS TO NEGLECT THEIR CHILDREN.

Jim and Sandi have found multiple rewards in pursuing their business venture. Financial success has not been the only prize.

"Horses," Jim said, "have taught me to relax and avoid the fast track. I work hard, but I don't work stressfully as so many business people do. I've watched the horses as they perform and I've been inspired by them. They execute with such grace and determination. It's a lesson for all of us, to remain more at peace and to live life more slowly."

Sandi too, has found similar rewards.

"Her love for the mares", Jim said, "and caring for the babies, has given her satisfaction that I can't fully appreciate."

Jim has found other outlets bring similar satisfaction.

JIM & SANDI BLUMER

"I'm active in my church," Jim said. "I don't neglect the spiritual part of life. For fun, I like a round of golf. But overall, it's the horses that fill my life.

"Sandi and I both have learned what a magnificent bond there is between humans and animals. For us, our horses aren't just a job, they are an outlet, where we find peace and communion."

< 3 7 >

CINDY BOWLING GARNER

THE ULTIMATE SUCCESS STORY

Building a successful business is not an overnight achievement. Ask any of America's entrepreneurs and they will tell you that the road to success is a steep uphill climb cluttered with unforeseen obstacles.

Ask Cindy Bowling Garner and she will tell you more.

Cindy will tell you that you must work hard, be ready to face incredible odds and risk all that you have to meet your objective. She will also tell you that you must fully believe in yourself and your enterprise with an obstinate commitment.

She will tell you, too, that you must conduct your business with the highest moral and ethical standards. She will tell you, finally, that you must have help along the way and that you must never forget

< 39 >

those who stood by your side cheering you on.

Cindy owes much of her success to her own drive and enthusiasm, coupled with a great love for horses.

"I was raised on a Wisconsin dairy farm." she said. "I prayed for a horse of my own, but my parents wouldn't give me one.

> "THEY HAVE HELPED ME BUILD MY LIFE."

"When I was 4 years old they took me to the fair and put me on the pony ride. I rode forever, and when it was time to go threw a tantrum and almost tore down a concession stand.

"When I was fourteen, I had saved some money and was able to buy my first horse. From there on I've always had horses. They have helped me build my life."

Cindy's success story is one filled with challenge. She and her late husband, John Bowling, struggled to build a profitable horse-breeding farm, but quickly found themselves owners of a losing enterprise. John had immense experience and a respected name in the breeding industry, but operating costs had escalated and sales weren't what they might have been. The 160-acre farm owned by the couple was home to about 150 head of horses, but cost of feed and transportation was immense and contributed heavily to their loss factor.

"We sat out in the front yard one day and faced the truth," Cindy said. "We were going broke. 'What's going to become of us?' we had to ask ourselves."

It was then that the Bowlings decided to concentrate on selling rather than breeding. They shifted their resources to a venture in consignment sales that would eventually become their financial salvation. But their new enterprise, Triangle Sales Company, Incorporated, was not launched without peril.

"Unfortunately we entered the business at a bad time, when the oil business and related economic conditions inflated horse prices," Cindy said. "In the first year we lost $80,000."

Cindy recalled the first sale they sponsored.

"It was a nightmare," she said. "It was March 1, at the Oklahoma City State Fair Grounds. We set up on a sunny Friday morning, but by five o'clock that evening the temperature plummeted to less than ten degrees and an ice storm began. By that time, less than half the cata-

<40>

loged 98 head of horses had arrived and most of the roads were impassable, including the Interstate. By the next morning the power was out in over half of the city, including the Holiday Inn where we were staying. It was freezing cold at the hotel, no hot water and no phone. It was hard to get out of bed while thinking about the disaster lying ahead of us.

"When we arrived at the fairgrounds, no additional horses had arrived. The sales arena wasn't heated and it was so cold the paint froze on the horses as we numbered them.

"One hour before the sale was supposed to start, (of course no one knew when that was to be because we forgot to put the starting time in the catalog) no one else was there except the few consignors that had managed to arrive before the storm. We were devastated and ready to quit."

Gordon Hannagan, their auctioneer, gave the Bowlings the heart to continue.

John told Gordy, "I think we should call this thing off."

But Gordy said, "Heck, no, you're already committed. If I were you, I'd go right ahead and take the risk."

John and Cindy heeded Hannagan's words and waited fearfully for the outcome.

"Five minutes before we were to begin," Cindy said, "a few people showed up, ran into the barn, looked at the horses and then scurried back to the warmth of their vehicles. When a horse they were interested in came into the ring, they would jump out, run in and bid, and then run back to stay warm. A few people even drove right into the barn."

THE BOX SCORE AT THE END OF THE DAY WASN'T GREAT, BUT HELD PROMISE.

The box score at the end of the day wasn't great, but held promise. Of the 23 buyers who showed up, all made purchases.

"I'm amazed that out of that list of 23," said Cindy, "many are still regular customers and old friends today. Despite the freezing weather, we ended up selling 80 percent of the horses that made it to the sale, which was remarkable. When we were ready to leave, John said solemnly, 'God sure takes care of dummies.'

"I have to agree. We made many stupid mistakes over those first

< 4 1 >

few years. We learned by trial and error and because we had excellent help."

Some of the best guidance came from Cindy's neighbor and fond friend, Karen Craighead.

"She was my mentor, and had years of experience in the horse sales arena," Cindy said. "Without her guidance we wouldn't be where we are today."

Despite the early growing pains, Triangle Sales Company has flourished and, after 20 years, has become a leader in the industry. In 1999, the company sold to every state in the union with sales exceeding $11 million. With six sales in their main location of Shawnee, Oklahoma and two others in Ardmore, Oklahoma, in 2000 Cindy sold more than 5,000 horses.

"We've tried to be innovative and ground-breaking," Cindy said. "We produce what I believe to be the finest and most comprehensive catalog in the industry. We use direct mail and I think we were the first consignment company to set up a web site on the Internet. Our advertising budget is enormous. We run ads in all the major journals, including Western Horse, Quarter Horse, Paint Horse, Quarter Horse News, Southern Horse and many others."

'GOD SURE TAKES CARE OF DUMMIES.'

Cindy takes pride in her business and work ethic.

"We pride ourselves on being fair and honest with our customers and buyers," She said. "We charge a reasonable consignment fee of $150 with an eight percent commission on the sale. The commission is waived if the horse isn't sold. We also want to know what we are doing wrong so that we can remedy any problem. We can't make everyone happy, but will try our best to do so."

The result of Cindy's philosophy is a thriving business that is worthy of pride. But her personal life has borne its share of losses. After the business began to achieve stability and growth, Cindy's husband of 18 years contracted leukemia and suffered a painful death.

Cindy moved forward, throwing her energies into the business and her farm in Shawnee. In 1996, she married Mike Garner, a well-known horseman and auctioneer. Mike left his home and auction busi-

< 4 2 >

ness in North Carolina to become Cindy's life partner and staunch supporter in her business efforts.

Mike, who began trading ponies when he was 7 years old, has an extensive background in the horse and sale business. Mike manages the breeding operation and assists Cindy at the sales and in the office with public relations, problem solving and good advice.

> "I'VE LEARNED A LOT FROM MY HORSES."

Today, Cindy enjoys the best of both worlds, spending half of her time on the farm and the remainder managing her business. She has found time to garden, make preserves and dry her home-grown herbs. She is also active in her church and supports community projects. She allows her employees paid time off to assist at the town's annual junior rodeo.

"I've learned a lot from my horses," Cindy said. "They have taught me to be patient and genuine in dealing with them and with life in general. Horses are supremely intelligent. They recognize love and can sense insincerity in their owners and handlers. They can quickly spot a phony. That's why I've elected to conduct my business with sincerity and honesty.

"It's the familiar spiritual theme of doing unto others as you want them to do unto you that works in life. That's what God wants us to do. We put God first, and look at what has happened."

< 4 3 >

HOME ON THE RANGE

Every time Madelon Leonard Bradshaw looks at the tiny pair of cowboy boots on her office shelf, she fondly remembers the vigorous days of her early childhood when she rode horses every time her parents allowed.

"They still have mud on them and the heels are worn down, so I know they were mine," she said, chuckling. "Those boots are one of my treasured possessions."

Marvin Leonard, the legendary Fort Worth department store magnate, encouraged the youngest of his four daughters to enjoy horses. When Madelon was 4 years old, she would watch cowboy movies on television with her father and get inspired to ride.

She always looked forward to riding her brown and white

< 4 5 >

Shetland pony at the Forest Park Stables, just behind her father's Colonial Golf Club course. Boy, the name of the Shetland, always mischievously ran away with the 5-year-old Madelon to the point that she fell off his back every time she rode him. Determined, she kept getting back on the pony until she mastered "the little devil" at the age of 10.

> "KIDS TODAY WANT TO BE IMMEDIATELY GRATIFIED."

At 13, Madelon acquired a palomino mare named Miss Clover Buck. The horse, which followed her around the stables for the carrots she carried in her pocket, soon became her favorite. She showed the mare in the horsemanship and reining classes at exhibitions in Richland Hills, the Fort Worth Stock Show and the State Fair of Texas.

During her teen years, Madelon became interested in English riding when a lady allowed her to regularly exercise her jumper horse at the stables. She went to Montgomery, Alabama and bought a big thoroughbred that was trained as a hunter and to do dressage.

Fort Worth horse shows at that time did not often feature English riding classes. So Madelon enjoyed the experience of recreational riding with the Fort Worth Pony Club during her junior and senior years of high school. She became so attached to her thoroughbred that she took him with her to New York, where she attended her first year of college.

Madelon said that growing up around horses gave her a sense of responsibility.

"I learned that when you've got a horse, it's not like a baseball that you can leave in the closet, and the following year, when you want to use it, it's there," she said. "A horse needs to be taken care of on a daily basis. Kids today want to be immediately gratified. They don't understand that it takes responsibility and work to get there."

After living in Florence, Italy for three and a half years, Madelon came home to show Quarter Horses in the western pleasure and hunt seat classes during the '70s. In 1984, she and her husband bought a ranch between Fort Worth and Weatherford. It was there that one of the foremen working for them told Madelon about the fun of team roping.

This popular event came from the days when cowboys had to

< 46 >

team up to catch a sick cow, so they could treat it with medicine. The first roper, the header, ropes the head of the steer, and veers off to the left, while his partner, the heeler, ropes its hind feet.

Madelon sent one of her young mares to a trainer who quickly developed her into a team roping horse.

"Tippy is a fantastic mare," she said. "I don't ride her or go anywhere that people don't compliment me on how nice and pretty she is, and how well she is to rope off of. She gets me there and really takes care of me."

During a competition in the late '80s, a 600-pound steer tripped up the mare when she got too close. Madelon flipped off the horse and fell face first into the ground. She was rushed to Harris Hospital, where she spent the next two months recovering from a closed head injury. She said that she did not remember anything for three weeks after her accident.

Every weekend after Labor Day since the late '80s, to improve her skills Madelon has attended a team roping school taught by national champion Walt Woodard. Under his tutelage she courageously came back better than before her mishap.

"After my accident he [Woodard] helped me learn how to rope again and to stay safe," she said.

Despite her serious fall, Madelon still enjoys team roping for the fun of it.

"Winning is fun, but it's not the most important thing to me," she said. "I like doing what I set out to do, which is roping the steer's head."

MADELON STILL ENJOYS TEAM ROPING FOR THE FUN OF IT.

She has been awarded belt buckles twice, which was a novelty for her, having received only trophies during her teenage years.

"I find it a challenge to win belt buckles," Madelon said. "People always comment on them and it makes me feel good."

After Madelon divorced in 1986, she had to learn how to manage her ranch by herself. The Soil Conservation Service recommended that she rotate her cattle, so she went to grazing school and learned the proper techniques.

"It made perfect sense to me, because it reminded me of what my dad had done with the mowing of his golf course," she said. "On the

< 47 >

ranch, I put the cattle in a smaller pasture and let them graze on that area. The next day, I move them onto another area and allow the first pasture time to grow again."

For the conscientious upkeep of her 30 pastures, Madelon has received several grazing awards from the National Resource Conservation Service and the Society of Range Management.

"I take what I hear and learn about, and use the knowledge to make my place better," Madelon said. "I want to be a responsible conservator of the environment and leave the land better than when I found it."

The resourceful manager also puts her goats to work cleaning out the thick underbrush that covers part of the ranch. She said that they would eat the leaves as far as they can reach by standing on their hind legs.

"I'm using goats instead of a bulldozer, but it's definitely a slower process," she said, laughing.

Madelon began to raise chickens in the late '80s after visiting Virginia farmer Joel Salatin, whose pasture poultry operation was featured in The Stockman Grass Farmer. Basically, he has raised chickens in 10-foot square cages, moving them daily onto fresh grass as well as feeding them grain, and then selling them as broilers.

> "I WANT TO BE A RESPONSIBLE CONSERVATOR OF THE ENVIRONMENT AND LEAVE THE LAND BETTER THAN WHEN I FOUND IT."

Fascinated by the process, Madelon and her "business brain" went to work. She said that many people like the quality chickens she raises, which are fed grass and insects along with regular grain.

"These chickens are like the ones we ate 30 years ago, before they were raised in confinement houses," she said.

To learn even more, Madelon attended ranch management classes at Texas Christian University in Fort Worth, graduating in 1990. She continues to audit evening classes to keep up with innovations in the ranching industry.

She said ranching requires an extensive knowledge of what to do, how to do it and who to call to get help.

< 4 8 >

MADELON BRADSHAW

"The conclusion I've come to is that ranching is one of the most complicated businesses there is," Madelon said. "You're not just a rancher. You'd better know about livestock, nutrition, veterinary work, horticulture, plumbing, carpentry, electrical work and anything else that needs building or repairing."

Her secret of success involves adapting to different situations and keeping an open mind to new ideas and innovations.

"When the cows get out of the pasture, or the thunderstorm last night fried the charger on the electric fence, you have to stay flexible," she said.

< 4 9 >

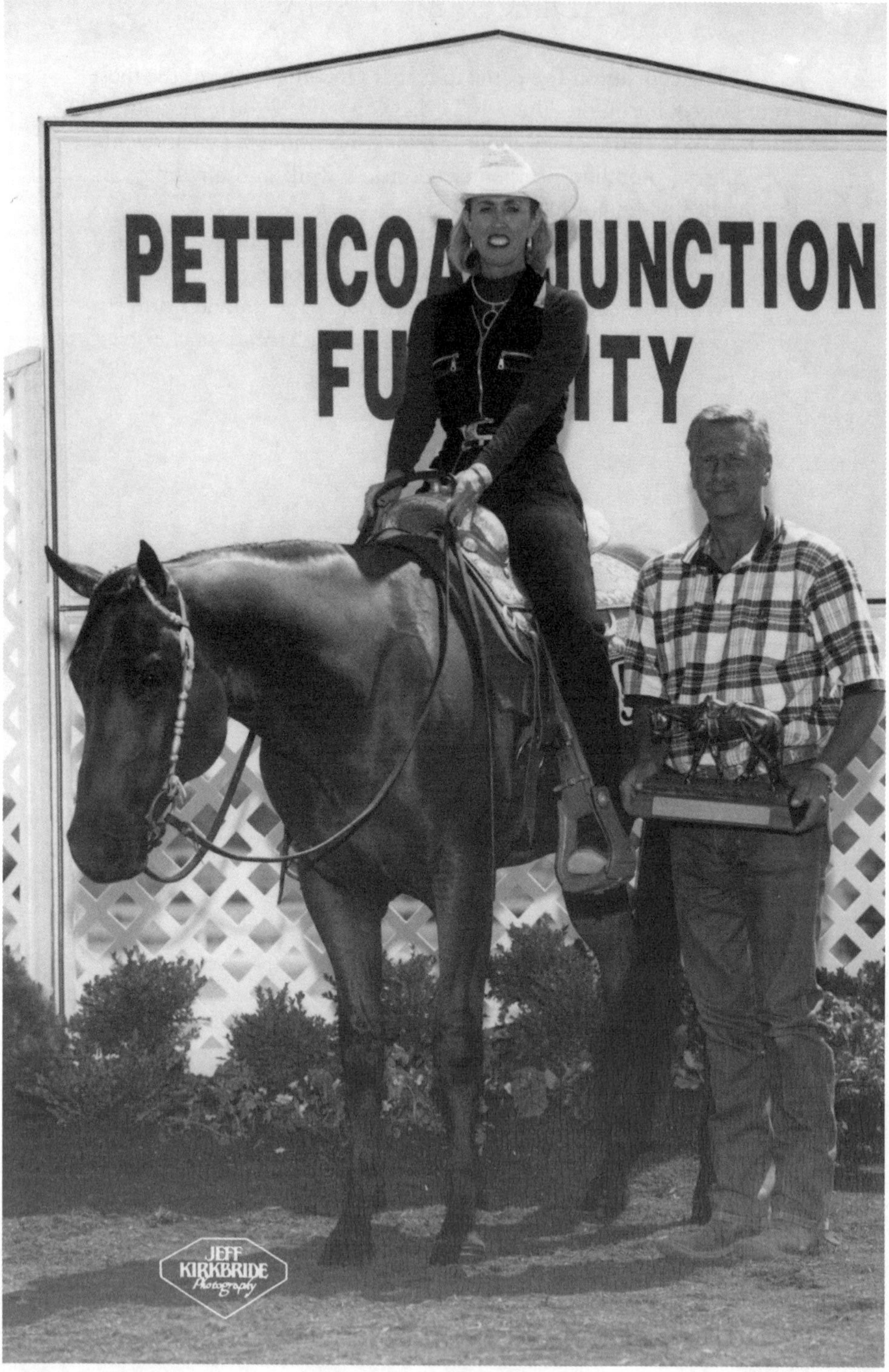
PETTICOA
UNCTION
FU
ITY
JEFF
KIRKBRIDE
Photography

DONNIE & MILLIE DICKERSON

A TEAM
EFFORT

Cooperative teamwork is vital to the success of a business, something North Carolina horse trainer Donnie Dickerson and his wife, Millie, discovered early on. Since 1971, they have managed a profitable operation – owning and selling western pleasure horses.

Donnie trains and sells the horses, while Millie and their son Taft (born in 1990) enjoy competing at horse shows across the country. In addition, Millie takes care of the daily paperwork and the bookkeeping. Donnie and Millie proudly value what each other contributes to the business.

"I always give Millie a lot of credit," Donnie said, "because she's been the one doing the showing. And it's worked out well. I've tried to support her with the best stock that I could."

< 51 >

Millie also appreciates her husband's efforts on her behalf.

"Donnie has always made sure that I had a competitive horse," she said, "and he always prepares it to the best of his ability."

The Dickersons grew up in the small country town of Mt. Airy, the hometown of actor Andy Griffith in the Mayberry RFD television series popular years ago and now in reruns. They went to the same school, but were not good friends until Millie's cousin helped them become acquainted.

THEY SHARED A COMMON INTEREST IN THEIR LOVE OF HORSES.

After they started dating the couple discovered that they shared a common interest in their love of horses. Millie's brother had gotten her horses ready for shows in the past, but Donnie accepted that responsibility after they got married.

On weekends Donnie rode in barrel racing competitions and Millie showed her pleasure horses. They own a farm just a half a mile from where each of them had lived during their childhood years.

During the early years of their marriage Donnie sold many kinds of horses, but eventually began specializing in western pleasure horses because of the great demand in the eastern states. He usually sells more than 100 head a year, and 95 percent of them are Western pleasure horses.

Donnie said he does not breed them simply because he doesn't have the time.

He recognized early on that some horses could not handle western pleasure riding because they were too active.

"If you have a horse that has a movement or energy of a cutting horse or a barrel horse, you would destroy him trying to make him into a western pleasure horse," he said. "Everybody thinks that training a horse in western pleasure is so easy, but it's really not because you have to ask him to do everything that he's not supposed to do. In western pleasure you hang the horse out there with a loose rein and make him go slow, but maybe he wants to gallop. It's just not in him to go slow."

Still, Donnie treasures the different personalities he observes in his horses.

"Individuality with horses is like individuality with people," he

<52>

said. "They all have their personalities and you have to treat them all differently."

Donnie has a never give up attitude when he trains horses.

"Because a horse is not performing up to par, you've got to believe in your heart that if you've picked out a prospect and told yourself that this is the one you're going to train you have to see it through many stages, both good and bad," he said. "People from all walks of life in this day and time give up too easily. Everyone has days that aren't as good as others. But as for me, I don't say I'm finished. I take a bit of pride in trying to make each horse the best that it can be. It might not be the winner, but hopefully I've turned out a good product in the end."

In the spring of 1999, Donnie was training a horse for upcoming competitions that didn't seem to be progressing as much as he liked. Millie had showed the horse on a few occasions, but was not satisfied that it was going to work for her. Taft, however, teamed up with this particular horse a month or so later and after a few shows had aspirations of showing him at the Congress in October 1999. Taft won with him, making Donnie feel as though his efforts had paid off in a very big way.

During the '80s, Millie participated in area American Quarter Horse Association (AQHA) shows with the family's favorite mare, Tuno Tag Leo, which in 2000 was 20 years old and is still at the Dickersons' farm. Tuno was the first horse that introduced Donnie and Millie to the world of AQHA competition. They had competed for many years at local open shows, but were looking forward to new ventures.

> DONNIE HAS A NEVER GIVE UP ATTITUDE WHEN HE TRAINS HORSES.

Tuno was the first in the line of many great talented horses for the Dickersons. Millie won the 2- and 3-year-old Non-Pro western pleasure snaffle bit classes at the 1999 All-American Quarter Horse Congress with Texas T Bone and Mr. Sugar Deluxe, respectfully. Taft won the Novice Youth Western Pleasure class with Par Te Major Fox.

Millie believes in mentally preparing for each event.

"My confidence in the ring comes from knowing my horse is

< 5 3 >

well-prepared and feeling that I have prepared for the moment, whether it's by wearing the outfit that makes me feel like I look the best or by knowing the silver has been cleaned on my saddle," she said. "People have always told me I look confident when I enter the arena, but I just go in thinking, 'This is what I love doing.'"

Millie also gratefully acknowledges all the people who have played a part in her accomplishments over the years.

"There are so many factors in the equation other than just me," Millie said. "I've always looked at my success in showing as being a result of the efforts of many people on my behalf. It requires a lot of people working together."

When the Dickerson children started competing, they sometimes got discouraged when they didn't win every time. Donnie and Millie encouraged them to simply do their best and accept what comes.

"There has to be a feeling somewhere along the line that there is something other than getting a blue ribbon," Millie said. "We've tried to tell our children many times that if they give it their best, no matter what they do in life, that's enough in itself."

THE CHILDREN HAVE LEARNED TO SET GOALS AND HAVE TRIED THEIR BEST TO ACHIEVE THEM.

The Dickersons' do appreciate the fact that through their participation in horse competitions the children have learned to set goals and have tried their best to achieve them.

Millie passed down her competitive spirit to her children. Daughter Jennifer (born in 1977) was a strong competitor in the show arena during her teenage years, having won the Congress in 1989 with Seven S Majestic and in 1992 with Make Me Sleepy. Then she took some time off after getting married and having a baby.

After a five-year break from showing, Jennifer was a finalist in the 3-year-old Non Pro western pleasure class at Quarter Horse Congress in 1999.

"She felt good about herself...that she was still able to be competitive and still had the desire to achieve," Millie said.

The couple is very proud of the accomplishments of both children in and out of the show arena.

Taft made the Congress youth team in 2000. Millie said he

< 5 4 >

DONNIE & MILLIE DICKERSON

"absolutely eats and sleeps horses," and has aspirations of one day becoming an AQHA judge and a horse trainer. He enjoys playing cowboys and Indians on his two ponies and miniature horse out in the fields, and also consistently rides on the show horses.

Because of the variety of events that are available at both local and national competitions, Millie recommends that families looking for a hobby should try showing horses. She said that working with horses has not only given her family a comfortable way of making a living, but it has kept she and her husband close to the children.

"We've had many memorable moments, and it's been a wonderfully exciting experience," said.

"In this day and time, I think it's hard to keep a family close," Donnie said. "Working with horses has been a way that we've stayed together in the good times and the bad times."

> MILLIE RECOMMENDS THAT FAMILIES LOOKING FOR A HOBBY SHOULD TRY SHOWING HORSES.

< 5 5 >

LATE BLOOMER

When Walt Downer was 35 years old, he was successfully operating a new car dealership and restoring classic cars in Elmer, New Jersey. Yet, he still felt something was missing from his life. He was not getting any emotional pay back from selling and fixing up inanimate objects. Instead, he wanted a more fulfilling career, one that he could pour his energy and efforts into and get an end result in the bargain. His mind drifted back to his childhood and he recalled that his most enjoyable moments were spent on the back of a horse.

Walt had never owned a horse because he had never wanted one. He had, however, been around horses during his childhood.

Just before Walt was born his parents and two older brothers brought back a couple of wild pony babies from the Chincoteague

< 57 >

auction in the back of their station wagon. They put them in the large fenced backyard where the boys "had a ball" taking care of them and watching them grow. When the horses got older, the brothers broke them out on a three-acre piece of property down the road and kept them there.

Then his father bought a couple more horses. Walt enjoyed riding these horses when he was 5 years old, but he had to share them with his brothers and cousins.

Following the death of his 60-year-old mother in 1993, Walt told his wife, Patti, that he was going to buy a couple of Quarter Horses. By the year 2000 he owned 100 Quarter Horses, does his own breeding along with some showing, and runs a 200-acre farm on the outskirts of the tiny hamlet.

> "IT'S A LOT OF WORK, WITH PLENTY OF SLEEPLESS NIGHTS."

The Downers have discovered that working on a farm is a full-time, never-ending job, especially during the hectic breeding season. Walt stays up at night to personally foal every mare on the farm.

"It's a lot of work, with plenty of sleepless nights," he said. "I guess I'm too hands-on, but I don't rely on employees for that."

He said he enjoys the breeding process because of the heart-warming end result of new quality foals.

For Patti, who was not raised on a farm, learning the breeding process was a big adjustment. She took classes, which helped her a great deal. She loves the challenge of getting mares in foal.

"In the beginning, our conception rate was low because we didn't listen to what the mares were telling us," Walt said. "Instead, we were listening to what the vets and clinicians were saying. Sometimes the mares will dictate when and how they'll be bred."

The Downers' horses now enjoy a high conception rate.

In July of 2000, Walt and Patti had a baby of their own, a cute little girl they named Kaitlyn. The couple had been married 20 years, but they had decided to wait before starting their family.

"When Walt found out I was pregnant, he said he wanted a girl because girls are more likely to be interested in horses than boys are," Patti said, laughing.

"I hope that our girl will compete in the youth horse events, but

<58>

I know that we won't force it on her," Walt said.

The Downers still own the car dealership in town, but Patti is primarily responsible for operating the business. Walt shows up at the dealership twice a day, but his focus is primarily on farm work.

"If it came down to it, I'd sell the dealership tomorrow," Walt said. "I don't know how financially sound the horse business will be in the future, but it's been OK for us."

Walt also sits on a local bank board, which he said keeps him occupied.

Patti prefers their new lifestyle in the country to living in the town, even though Elmer is a quaint, "one-stoplight" village where all the stores close at 5 p.m. and no alcohol is served. She said she likes wide, open spaces, so being able to own such a huge spread was a godsend.

"I love the room out here," she said, referring to the farm.

Walt said he enjoys every seasonal aspect of farm work, including the breeding work during the winter. He likes the haying and mowing in the spring, the mending of fences and general ranch duties in the summer, and the "breaking out" and preparation of the yearlings for the sales ring in the fall. He remembers, however, that he has to efficiently manage his farm business like he operates his car dealership.

> PATTI PREFERS THEIR NEW LIFESTYLE IN THE COUNTRY TO LIVING IN THE TOWN.

"We run this as a business, without question," Walt said. "The farm started out as a hobby, but because of the number of our head, we have to run it as a business."

Walt does have one favorite horse that has captured his heart; a 16-hand black stallion named Principle Investment. As a yearling, he has won such events in 1989 as the Congress Pleasure Futurity, The Texas Classic, The Solid Gold Futurity, and the Indiana State Fair Futurity. He was an American Quarter Horse Association Superior Pleasure Horse with 66 points and placed fourth in the 1989 World Show Two Year Old Snaffle Bit Futurity. Even though Principle's show career was over when he was 3 years old, he now stands at stud and produces championship quality

< 5 9 >

offspring that the Downers show.

Patti said Principle Investment is just as emotionally attached to Walt as Walt is to him.

> "WE ONLY ASK A LITTLE BIT EACH DAY FROM THEM."

"When Walt goes into the barn and Principle hears his voice, he perks up his ears and acts completely different," she said. "It would be hard for Walt to part with him."

Walt appears to have rapport, however, with all 100 horses, Patti said. He knows them all and has a special relationship with each one.

Walt said that in the beginning he wanted to show horses, so he found some trainers willing to teach him how to present them. He also learned from experience and the mistakes others made.

"We've been fortunate enough to have a lot of friends in the business," he said.

When Walt breaks out his foals, he prefers the gentle, easygoing approach.

"We are real easy with our animals," he said. "We don't ask too much of them or reprimand them. We only ask a little bit each day from them."

Walt said he realizes that his personality has changed quite a bit over the years.

"The horse business has mellowed me out," Walt said. "In the beginning I thought I could take an animal and within a few short sessions teach it to do something, but it didn't work. I realize now how much patience and virtue is involved. I have to let the horse dictate to me when it's ready to do whatever I'm asking, so I'm never in a hurry anymore."

< 6 0 >

DIXIE NATIONAL QUARTER HORSE SHO
Southern Class
DIXIE NATIONAL
2000
Dixie National
Quarter Horse Show
JACKSON, MISSISSIPPI
DIXIE NATIONAL
QUARTER HORSE SHOW
Sundowner
TRAILERS
Harold
Campton

JERRY FLEISNER & KATHI LAWRENCE

WORLD OF EXPERIENCE

When it comes to the horse business, Jerry Fleisner and Kathi Lawrence have discovered over the years that two heads truly are better than one. This is especially true for them, since they have almost 70 years of experience between them in breeding, training and showing horses.

Although they had known each other through a mutual friend since 1973, it was not until 1988 that they formed a limited partnership and bought a 50-acre horse ranch in central Oklahoma. Their specialty on the 88 Bar Limited Ranch is developing Quarter Horse foals and showing them in futurity competitions around the country. By pooling their skills and years of experience, they have been quite successful.

< 6 3 >

"Jerry and I are a good team," Kathi said. "We complement each other in our business. I'm the one who trains the foals and gets them to stand. He takes them and shows them. It takes a certain knack to show them in the arena and he's very good at that."

"WE TREAT THEM LIKE FAMILY AND WE GET ALONG."

When Kathi encounters a foal that is too much for her, she hands it over to Jerry. He sees them like children who have difficulty learning in school.

"Sometimes it takes a little longer to train a foal," he said. "Some fall into the act and some don't, but they usually fall into place. If you treat the horses well, they're going to return it. If you're constantly picking on them they'll let you know they don't like it. We treat them like family and we get along."

Kathi thinks her genetic makeup causes her to want to bond with her horses. She has such a close connection with her brood mares that she can call them from the other end of the pasture and they come running.

She also views herself as a personal fitness trainer for individual horses. In her training pen she has chosen not to use traditional methods, such as those that involve walkers or lunging. Instead, she leads the foals behind either a golf cart or a John Deere utility vehicle so that they are not constantly going around in circles.

She also does what she can to improve their overall physical appearance by brushing them down and bathing them with hot oil to enhance hair quality. Under her careful scrutiny they are developed into potential champions.

"I pose them as if they were in a show and work on certain areas until I can mold them into what I think they should be," she said. "When I get into the show pen I hope that I have a foal that's the best one there. Some are just born to be show horses in that they have a certain charisma that attracts attention."

In August of 2000 the couple's 1400-pound mare, At Long Last Cool, was so well prepared for the American Quarter Horse Association Youth World Show that two judges told them that when she came through the gate, it was as if she was the only mare in the pen.

Not only does the horse have a championship presence in the

<64>

ring, but she also has an outgoing personality that enchants her public. She, Jerry and Kathi nicknamed her Snoopy, "because she snoops around in your pockets and has to know everything that's going on."

"We have strangers ask about her," Kathi said. "We see them and they ask about how Snoopy's doing. She has her own fan club."

Jerry said At Long Last Cool is one of the best horses they have had in a long time.

"When a good horse like her comes along, it keeps me motivated," he said. "I just know when I have a good one. It's like drivers at a NASCAR competition who are getting beat, but all of a sudden, their car is running just right."

Jerry has passed on his love for competition to his four children and 11 grandchildren. Abbie, his middle grandchild, won the 2000 Youth World with At Long Last Cool. He said his grandchildren always look forward to showing their horses on the weekends.

"Kids who are involved in horse shows keep themselves occupied," Jerry said. "They also learn about competing with other people, which happens in real life every day."

Being successful in the horse business has allowed Jerry and Kathi to meet people from all over the world. The partners have raised horses that have gone on to be exported to Brazil and Germany. He said he enjoys meeting interesting people who have a "good eye for horses."

The partners make sure their customers are buying top-quality foals by insisting on very high ethical standards. They belong to an association that has a strict code of ethics and the partners take their membership seriously.

> "KIDS WHO ARE INVOLVED IN HORSE SHOWS KEEP THEMSELVES OCCUPIED."

"If you can't represent your product honestly in this industry, you won't have any repeat business," Kathi said. " The people involved in the association are a close-knit group. People who don't stand by their word are weeded out. I've always believed that if you can't be held accountable for your word you're not worth too much. We do the best we can to represent our animals, not only in the show ring but also in our sales."

She also enjoys the mystery and wonder surrounding the births

<65>

of their new foals each year, because they may have another champion in the offing.

"Every year when it's time for the mares to have their foals, it's like Christmas," Kathi said. "We don't know what is going to come out of the package. Sometimes it's not exactly what we want and other times the foals exceed our expectations. We try to be with each mare when she foals and it's always a surprise."

She said that sometimes heartbreak comes along with foaling. One year a mare was just a few days away from giving birth. She didn't look quite right, so the partners took her to the vet. The mare didn't act distressed and foaled. Although everything looked normal, she passed away and her foal also died.

"We try to catch things before they get out of hand by doing our own preventative vet work and spending more time with the horses," Kathi said. "When you deal with a living being, though, sometimes you don't have control. That's part of the heartache that goes with the job."

> "WE TRY TO CATCH THINGS BEFORE THEY GET OUT OF HAND."

Despite the sadness they occasionally experience the partners said they love what they do and cannot see working in any other occupations.

After growing up on a dairy farm in Wisconsin, Jerry followed his father into the construction and plumbing business and was licensed as a master plumber. And at one time Kathi made artificial human heart valves for the University of Minnesota, a job that carried a great responsibility with it because, she said, "If you make a mistake, someone dies."

The partners, however, had grown up around horses, so the siren call to raise horses proved to be irresistible.

"Both Jerry and I have tried to do other things, but we've always come back to working with horses," Kathi said. "We just couldn't stay away."

< 6 6 >

< 67 >

GREATER THAN GREAT

"On the fifth day, God created horses." – Genesis 1:24

Lana Gabriel is quickly becoming a rising star in the world of quarter horses. Asked about her success, she is quick to say that it is a team effort and that the man responsible for putting her in the winner's circle is husband, Ron.

"When I met Ron I knew absolutely nothing about horses," Lana said. "In fact, I didn't even know how to put a halter on a horse. He introduced me to horses soon after we met. Prior to that I knew more about my car's horsepower than I did about the power of a horse."

When Lana met Ron she was living in Dallas managing the

< 69 >

world's largest company in the photographic processing equipment business. Living life in the fast lane, Lana was always running from meeting to meeting, traveling from state to state and working long hours. In short, her job was her life.

Ron was also on the corporate fast track. He was a successful businessman who ran several companies simultaneously. However, Ron was a country gentleman, too.

FOR THE GIRL FROM THE CITY, IT WAS LOVE AT ITS BEST.

Though much of his life had been spent around horses, and while he enjoyed the lifestyle associated with them, Ron considered horses more a sideline and serious hobby. Little did he know that his wife-to-be would not only fall madly in love with him, but also with horses. For the girl from the city, it was love at its best.

"When Ron took me to my first horse show, the AQHA World Show," she said, "I was impressed with the halter discipline and decided then and there that it was something I wanted to do myself. I immediately recognized my desire and attraction to horses, and Ron made my dream of working with them come true."

In 1992 Lana took her first step toward realizing her dream when, after taking a three-week crash course on how to show a horse, she and Obviously Taurus walked away from the TAQHA show with an Amateur Grand Championship win.

In her first halter class show Lana won a Grand. And during her short show career she has won numerous prestigious championship titles nationwide. She is especially proud of her "multiple" World Championship titles and "multiple" Reserve World Championship titles. Among these titles she has a Solid Gold win with a weanling stallion that she and her husband had raised.

Ron named this young stallion Clu Heir and recognized that the horse was special and unique when it was at a very young age. His ability to recognize talent proved correct when he and Lana took the colt to the AQHA World Championship Show and took two AQHA World Championship titles. These wins elevated the couple and the horse to elite status.

"Clu Heir is an incredible individual and has now proven himself as an outstanding sire," Lana said. "By the end of his 5th year of age, young for industry standards, his get had won four World Championship titles and four Reserve World Championship titles.

"Because I am the one who shows our horses and am most visible, I feel that oftentimes Ron does not get the credit he deserves," Lana said. "I could not have done this without him. He provided the knowledge, insight, love and friendship that are required. He has taught me so much. He is vital to our operation."

Lana said the halter discipline is distinctive.

"Horses are judged on confirmation and discipline," she said. "Many events have the benefit of being timed and the clock determines the winner. Halter is strictly the opinion of the judge(s) for the class. And the halter show horse is bred, groomed and trained like no other horse."

The thrill of victory was all it took for Lana to take a giant leap of faith. She literally changed horses mid stream. She went from having dreams of being a corporate mover and shaker to visions of standing in the winner's circle with a champion horse by her side.

"Ron raised and showed horses for 20 years before I met him," she said. "He was successful with his breeding decisions and successful in fitting, training and showing. During these years he also followed his entrepreneurial spirit and started a company unrelated to horses.

> "RON IS AN UNBE-LIEVABLY BRILLIANT BUSINESS MAN."

"Ron is an unbelievably brilliant business man. He does his research, knows the limits on which to base decisions, trusts and empowers those who are deserving, protects his employees, accepts responsibility and shares the glory.

"He's also generous and a great mentor to me. He loves our family and is an exceptional father and grandfather, but the first quality that I saw in him...the one that I admired most...is that he is a Christian. I truly admire his ability to balance the challenges of today's world without compromising his faith."

Together Ron and Lana make a great team. She is by nature competitive. And when she involved herself in showing horses, it was a total commitment.

<71>

"We started out with a couple of brood mares, bred them to appropriate stallions and I showed the foals," Lana said. "I truly enjoyed my initial experience but soon realized that my passion was not parallel with my skills. And on the level at which we were competing, skill is vital.

Driven by the desire to be the very best, Lana learned as much as possible about her new profession. Ron exposed her to every opportunity available, something he continues to do even now. So she went back to school, taking specialized courses, and eventually the student became the teacher.

Lana quickly realized that the road to fame with horses did not always lead to fortune. The champion exhibitor said breeding horses and preparing them for show is an expensive business – one that requires understanding in order to turn a profit.

After an evaluation of their horse business, Ron and Lana put their collective minds together and decided their brood mare herd had reached the quantity level where it would benefit them to purchase a breeding stallion of their own.

> "TO BE SUCCESSFUL WE NEEDED TO HAVE OUR OWN STALLION FOR BREEDING."

"As I said before, Ron has an exceptionally keen mind for business," Lana said, "and we both realized that to be economically successful we needed to have our own stallion for breeding. I told Ron that I knew I could handle it. So I enrolled myself in a crash course at Texas A & M University and learned how to properly collect stallions and artificially inseminate mares. I returned home and immediately started collecting the stallions and actively inseminating the mares myself. That was seven years ago and I haven't looked back."

Ron and Lana purchased a stallion with an impeccable pedigree – two-time world champion, Cool Me Down. He has bragging rights of his own.

"After we got Cool Me Down, Ron hand picked and purchased a mare specifically for him," Lana said. "The mare we purchased was in foal to a stallion that at the time was the nation's leading sire of sires, Obvious Conclusion. This mare, Just An Heiress, produced two-time world champion, Clu Heir.

<72>

RON & LANA GABRIEL

"After starting and dedicating time to our own breeding program, I didn't show horses for almost two years. Then Clu Heir came into our lives and Ron said that I should show him at the 1995 AQHA World Show. The World Show is the Super Bowl, Masters and Olympics all rolled into one for quarter horse enthusiasts. Prior to that I had only shown at smaller venues.

"Ron encouraged me to show at the World Show. He sent me into the arena with Clu Heir and we walked out with the Gold World Champion trophy."

Lana said that it was a couple of years later before she fully realized how important the event was to their program.

THERE IS NO SUCH THING AS A SECOND PLACE WINNER.

"Ron trusted me enough to put everything on the line that day," she said. "And while I knew it was important, I didn't realize how much that victory would change our lives. It caused me to later adopt the philosophy that there is no such thing as a second place winner. It's all or nothing. This philosophy is representative of my competitive approach.

"Our success today is a direct result of winning that event. I will always appreciate Ron for the chance he was willing to take by putting me on the lead shank and sending me into the arena with Clu Heir."

After stunning the horse community and breeders of numerous champion horses with their unparalleled successes, Lana and Ron continue their winning ways by having one of the highest conception rate breeding barns in the country. From February through July each year they run hundreds of mares through their breeding program.

Lana being the driving force behind the breeding program, and Ron's uncanny ability to identify a good horse, translates into good business.

"Ron has an excellent eye for horses," Lana said. "You have to be a shrewd business person to make money in this industry and that is where a lot of people make mistakes. He is also excellent with pedigrees and confirmation. Ron can take one look at a mare and know exactly what kind of stallion she should be bred to. I can't even begin to express how important that is to our business. "

< 7 3 >

An innovator by nature, Lana has opened a door to their breeding program that allows mares to be inseminated by their champion stallions without ever having to leave home.

FACING NOTHING BUT GREEN PASTURES, THE GABRIELS ARE LIVING A LIFESTYLE THEY BOTH LOVE.

"Initially all quarter horse mares had to be serviced at the breeding ranches," Lana said. "A few years ago the AQHA passed a regulation that allows us to ship semen. I learned how to prepare it properly for shipping. Our clients can now impregnate their mares without hauling them across the country."

Facing nothing but green pastures, the Gabriels are living a lifestyle they both love. Both continue to fulfill their dreams while establishing new goals for their future.

When Lana reflects on the whirlwind of success they've had, versus the life she once lived, a smile sneaks its way onto her face followed by a sigh of relief.

"I can't begin to express how fortunate I am to have met Ron," she said. "In addition to being a wonderful husband it was because of him that I am doing something that I dearly love...working with horses. I didn't realize that I loved animals so much.

"And no one could have convinced me years ago that I would be living on a ranch, breeding and showing champion horses. Thanks to having Ron, I have received many blessings from knowing these incredible animals. The horses we own have a great life and, as we say at Gabriel Quarter Horses, there is a difference between being good and great.

"But greater than great is how much I love Ron."

<74>

<75>

DENNIS HARRIS

GOD, OIL AND HORSES

Dennis Harris was not born on a horse, but got on one as quickly as he could.

By the time he was 4 years old, he was a serious rider – and his folks were living in Lovington, New Mexico where an oil boom was in full swing. Because his father was a minister who started First Christian churches (170 during his lifetime), Harris got to know most of the ranchers in the area – and they all had horses for him to ride.

"I can't remember a time when I didn't enjoy being around horses," he said, "and there were plenty of them in West Texas and New Mexico where my dad started so many churches. I rode with ranchers, oil men and old cowboys who had settled the area when they were just kids…when everybody still wore a holster with a six-shooter in it."

<77>

Harris did not like what his dad did, because it was almost impossible to form any sort of attachment to the people with whom he came in contact. As soon as his father got a congregation going, he was off to start another – and, of course, the family went with him.

By the time he was 14, when not in school, Harris worked as a roustabout in the oil fields. And he also worked on ranches.

> "ONE OF THE THINGS I LEARNED IS THAT YOU CAN'T BE FREE AND WORK FOR SOMEONE ELSE."

"I watched, listened and learned," he said. "I was around oil field workers and people who had a lot of money. Some of those people had 30,000-acre ranches and lots of oil wells. They had what I wanted...because one of the things I learned is that you can't be free and work for someone else."

At least a part of Harris' desire for financial independence, he thinks, was because his father was a bivocational minister who rarely received any more from a church than a parsonage and "tip money." He supported his ministry by working, which Harris thinks is probably more New Testament than the corporate way many churches operate today.

Though his family's moving around and his weekend work had a definite impact on Harris' extracurricular school activities, he ran track and was on golf and rodeo teams in high school.

Following graduation from high school, Harris attended Lubbock Christian College and then Texas Tech University, both in Lubbock, Texas. While admitting that academically he was less than stellar as a student, he was an intercollegiate rodeo champion – a bull and bareback rider – at Tech.

Harris dropped out of college in '62 and joined the Army because "everybody was getting drafted." He also married his sweetheart, Kay, who lived in Eunice, New Mexico.

"Some women throw cold water on your dreams," Harris said, "but Kay always supported mine. Even when she knew they probably wouldn't materialize, she supported my efforts. And even during my six years in the Army, I had big dreams."

When Harris got out of the Army in '68, his big dreams were put

< 7 8 >

on hold. He and Kay moved back to the West Texas-New Mexico area where he drove an oil field truck. It was during this period that he experienced a transformation that dramatically changed his life.

"I was angry and not a very nice person," he said. "I had all this head knowledge about the Bible, but I wasn't a Christian. Kay, of course, never wavered from her faith, but she didn't push me. She just prayed and set an example of how you can lead by following...kind of like making cattle think it's their idea to go in a certain direction.

"Anyway, she got me to a Baptist encampment where I discovered what Christ was all about and it turned my life around. There was such a dramatic change in me that pastors of various churches started asking me to give my testimony. That wasn't hard for me because moving around all those years when I was a kid had made it easy for me to meet people...and there sure wasn't any stage fright on my part. So I went all over the country preaching and teaching."

Harris' conversion caused him to enroll in Southwestern Baptist Theological Seminary in Fort Worth, Texas, where he studied theology and served as a staff evangelist for Wedgewood Baptist Church – the church that was in the media spotlight in 1999 when a crazed gunman went on a killing spree.

After a couple of years Harris' wanderlust took him to Montana to help build a church, then back to Brackettville, Texas to serve as chief of security at Fort Clark Springs. He soon became general manager and friend of a multimillionaire who asked him to move to Dallas to help with a startup company.

> HARRIS' WANDERLUST TOOK HIM TO MONTANA TO HELP BUILD A CHURCH.

"Looking back I can see God's hand in all of this," he said, "but I didn't always see it at the time. Anyway, when I got to Dallas I helped start the company and met people who had invested in oil deals...and they asked me to look at their paperwork. That led me back into the oil business...and I explored and drilled wells all over Texas, Oklahoma, New Mexico and Colorado."

Harris' success in the oil business might best be validated by a story carried by the Dallas-Fort Worth media in 1983. He was the unidentified businessman who bid $97 million for the National

<79>

Football League's Dallas Cowboys. Though his bid was higher than that of Bum Bright, to whom the franchise was sold, powers within the organization feared the changes he was going to make.

"The truth is that I wasn't that interested in the Cowboys," he said. "I wanted Valley Ranch (real estate owned by the organization)."

Things changed dramatically for Harris with the "crash" in '86. He lost $30 million and had only $11,000 in the bank after paying bills. From life on a 14-acre estate, luxury automobiles and airplanes, he moved to Allen, Texas and bought a house with no money down.

And kept going.

Not willing to let his investors simply lose their money, Harris formed a publicly held company to save their investment. It took 14 years to get it up and running, but the company is now involved in numerous projects on an international level.

As for Harris, he's still in the oil and gas business – but he takes care of that business by telephone from his ranch near Fredericksburg, Texas. His hands-on business, his real love, is cattle and horses.

Pointing to a young colt, Harris said, "You see that baby there…weighs maybe 100 pounds…nothing but raw potential. I can make it anything I want it to be, but it's important that I let it show me what it wants to be. And you have to start out with good blood."

"IT'S IMPORTANT THAT I LET IT SHOW ME WHAT IT WANTS TO BE."

Harris has a dozen brood mare quarter horses, but is adding a half dozen thoroughbred brood mares and a half dozen performance brood mares to his stable.

"The key for someone like me is to find the best people in this business, who really know it, and to take their advice…which I've done. I learned in the military that a good leader knows when to delegate and when to stay out of the way."

Harris uses his business and investments to fund his ministry. He is founder of Lifeline World Mission and operates a far-reaching ministry of missions, evangelism and Bible conferences. A longtime advocate for abused children, he is author of 14 children's books.

His concern for children in the Gaza Strip resulted in him organ-

< 80 >

izing a peace conference that brought together every Palestinian political faction – something that had never been done before. He also produced a film about the Gaza Strip – and now provides sewing machines for women living there and computers for the area's schools. He also supports ministry projects in the Yucatan peninsula of Mexico and in Romania.

"Even during the financially tough times, Kay faithfully tithed," Harris said. "She never wavered in her stewardship, even when I did.

"The truth is that if I leave my kids and grandchildren $50 million and they don't know Jesus Christ as their Lord, I've failed. I want them to remember that I lived for Christ. And though I love raising horses, in everything I do, I want to make a mark for the kingdom of God."

> "EVEN DUR-
> ING THE
> FINANCIALLY
> TOUGH
> TIMES, KAY
> FAITHFULLY
> TITHED."

<81>

JULIE & GLEN HATCHETT

WAFFLE IRONS, & TOASTERS

Julie Hatchett has loved animals for as long as she can remember. Visits to her grandmother's farm near Collierville, Tennessee introduced her to the bounty of the barnyard and all its creatures. Early recollections are of a menagerie of animals that she would gather and bring home to her patient and understanding parents.

Keeping animals was difficult for Julie and her family because they lived in the city. Her father, though raised on farms, was a cotton broker who earned his living in Memphis, near Collierville. Despite location, however, Julie managed to maintain a home for the critters she accumulated.

"Once I found a pig," she recalled," and couldn't wait to take it home and care for it. At one time I had eleven stray dogs. I don't think

< 83 >

our neighbors were too happy about all my animal friends."

Julie, one of six children, was the maverick of the clan – always fascinated with stray critters, as opposed to brothers and sisters who held more pristine childhood pursuits. She was always ready to get down in the mud and mire with her animal charges.

JULIE'S FIRST HORSE CAME ALMOST BY ACCIDENT AND COULD HAVE BEEN A HEN INSTEAD.

Julie's first horse came almost by accident and could have been a hen instead. Her parents were involved with Les Passé, an organization that sponsors children with special needs. Her mother was in charge of an auction designed to raise money and her dad assisted by attending the event and helping to raise the bids.

As often happens at such events, he got stuck with a number of useless items – including several toasters and waffle irons. Since 11-year-old Julie accompanied him, he was badgered to fill her needs as well. Her initial focus was on a gamecock someone had donated. And she begged her father to win it for her. He reluctantly agreed. But when the bidding reached $25, he declined.

"I'm not paying more than $25 for a chicken," he told his tearful daughter.

That didn't stop Julie. When a chubby pony was led to the auction block, she was transfixed.

She said, "I remember yanking on my daddy's coattails and saying, 'I'll never ask for another thing daddy, I promise. I promise'"

That night, Julie became the proud owner of a $105 pony. Although her parents suspected the animal was pregnant, Julie claimed she was "only fat" and, guessing correctly, she brought the animal's weight down with exercise, loving care and a regimented diet.

"I named her Boots," Julie recalled, "I boarded her in town and rode her until I was 13 and my feet dragged on the ground."

A few years later Julie was given another horse, a birthday present from her parents.

"I called him Bet You Money," Julie said. "I boarded him in town and learned to ride like a pro."

Bet You Money introduced Julie to the world of jumping. She

< 8 4 >

entered numerous competitions, showed horses, won prizes and bought more horses of her own.

As Julie progressed through her youthful years, she failed to stray from her posture as an animal loving person. While her brothers and sisters matured and moved ahead in school and career pursuits, Julie remained in pigtails and blue jeans, always ready to befriend some new addition to her animal entourage.

Her parents grew concerned and tried to interest Julie in a more normal lifestyle, but Julie prevailed. She quit school early and took a job in a Collierville western goods store. Selling farm and ranch paraphernalia suited her style and led her eventually to buy the store, but the lure of farming and having a place of her own beckoned. Julie finally sold the store and invested in a country homestead near Collierville.

Although animals were her focus, Julie had inherited another love from her parents. Their involvement in Les Passé and the needs of special children rubbed off on Julie. She found a second love in caring for kids of all ages; particularly those challenged by physical or mental disabilities. With her twin love for animals and children, Julie established her farm as a haven for kids to visit and rediscover nature and all its domestic inhabitants.

She called her place Happy Times Farm, which soon became an educational retreat where children learned to care for animals. Every domestic species was included – chickens, ducks, calves, cows, ponies, horses, sheep and goats.

And though Julie focused on special needs children, it wasn't long before she realized a great truth.

SHE FOUND A SECOND LOVE IN CARING FOR KIDS CHALENGED BY PHYSICAL OR MENTAL DISABILITIES.

"All children have special needs of one kind or another," she said.

She then opened the farm to children of all ages, challenged or not, allowing them not only to learn from the animals but also to learn from one another.

"We hosted a young boy with spinal bifida," Julie said, "and despite his disability, he was accepted by all the children. I found that the farm taught more than just a love for animals. It taught the children to love one another as well."

< 8 5 >

Her farm became a Mecca for children, a place where they could work together to learn the wonders of nature and the serenity of life on a farm.

Julie's personal life didn't suffer either. She met and married husband, Glen, a city boy who had, like Julie, developed a love for the country and horses. Glen made the farm his home, but retained a thriving construction business, remodeling hotels and universities.

Children came – a daughter, Jody, who became Julie's twin in her love for animals, and a son, Robert, likewise absorbed the family-farming legacy.

Julie's love for horses grew with the years and the farm eventually expanded into a breeding center. She changed the name to Double H Farm and began a serious venture into the raising of Quarter Horses.

Glen and Julie have raised a number of prize winners that have earned them a revered place in the show horse world. TMF Double, a favorite black stallion won a 1998 Reserve Quarter Horse championship.

> "YOU LEARN ALONG THE WAY HOW WELL PEOPLE AND ANIMALS COMMUNE."

The Hatchett children continue to carry the family's horse raising banner forward. Jody consistently wins myriad competitions and son Robert now trains horses in a Florida location.

Julie enjoys the family's success but is happier in finding fulfillment from raising horses and managing her farm.

"You learn along the way how well people and animals commune and how difficult it is not to love and respect the animal kingdom," she said.

This truth came home to Julie in a most dramatic way a few years ago when returning from a buying trip to North Carolina. She, a friend and young son, Robert, were riding in a van towing a trailer containing two newly purchased horses and a caged dog. Suddenly the van's engine malfunctioned and caught fire, stranding the pair in the middle of a busy Interstate highway.

"I was terrified," Julie said. "Everything happened so fast. I thought van, trailer, horses and all of us would be consumed by the flames or killed in an explosion, but suddenly there was help all around us."

Passing truck drivers and car passengers saw the blazing vehicle

<86>

and stopped to pull them from the van. Help came from all quarters. Two truckers blocked the highway in both directions, then radioed other nearby truckers for assistance. The truck drivers immediately helped remove the horses and dog from the trailer that was almost consumed by the blaze. Nameless passers-by jumped to the rescue also, helping tether the horses and calm them while more help was summoned. Rescue vehicles were soon on the scene.

"The van was burned to a cinder, but the trailer, horses and all of us were safe," Julie said. "The horses, the dog, my friend, my son and I were helped by an army of compassionate people who seemed to come from nowhere and everywhere. Before I knew it, they were gone. Before I could even offer thanks.

> "BEFORE I KNEW IT, THEY WERE GONE. BEFORE I COULD EVEN OFFER THANKS."

"I've always been touched by that event. I was overwhelmed with the people who came to our rescue that day and how they cared. I've also learned something from horses and other animals I've come to love. I've come to realize how fragile life is for all of them, how dependent upon us they are. I've learned too that our compassion for each other and our animals is related. I discovered on that frightening day that there is a lot of good in people – a lot more good than there is bad."

< 8 7 >

EDDIE & ELISHA HICKS

LOVE ON HORSEBACK

Falling in love on horseback may not be everyone's idea of romance, but for Eddie and Elisha Hicks it was reality.

Horses were part of growing up for this young couple, so it wasn't unusual that their first date took place at a horse show. Both were in their early teens and the pair had been showing horses for several years.

Elisha, born and raised near Dunn, North Carolina in the heart of the state's farm and ranch country, said she could always remember having horses.

"My grandfather had a pony farm where people could come to ride them," she said. "My aunts and my mother kept horses and my Mom rode a horse up to a week before I was born. I was almost born

< 8 9 >

on horseback."

Eddie was born in Youngsville, just 60 miles north of Dunn. His parents also kept a typical farm.

"We had horses all our lives," Eddie recalled. "My mother and father took me to horse shows from the time I was 6, which was about the same time I began to ride."

The couple dated through their teens and only parted when it came time for college and career decisions.

Eddie attended Wake Technical School and became a tool and die maker. He opened his own business in Smithville, near Dunn, but continued showing horses as a sideline.

> **LOVE BLOOMED ANEW AND THE PAIR MARRIED IN 1996.**

Elisha, graduated from Westland College and took a job in Raleigh as a computer hardware engineer with a company called Altech. She ultimately bought a farm near Dunn, where the couple re-united.

Love bloomed anew and the pair married in 1996 on the 20th anniversary of their first date.

"It was our love for horses that brought us together again," Elisha said.

Eddie closed his tool and die making shop and joined his wife in what became their joint career – raising horses.

Eddie and Elisha now run a successful horse farm near Dunn. They specialize in halter Quarter Horses and stood five stallions in 2000, breeding 125 mares. Both continue to show horses and Elisha frequently rides in competition, having been written up in Southern Quarter Horse magazine.

Their work on the farm isn't their only activity. They serve as directors for the Quarter Horse Association of North Carolina.

Their daughter, Sarah, born in 1986, was also bitten by the equestrian bug and is an avid horsewoman. She has ridden and shown horses with her mother and father since she was 9.

"We sure love our horses," Elisha said. "I still work at Altech and have to drive an hour each way to Raleigh every weekday, but I help out on the farm when I get home in the afternoon and on weekends.

< 9 0 >

It's hard work, but it's relaxing, too. Being with the horses is my quiet time."

Running a horse farm isn't an easy vocation, Eddie said.

"Every day is different, but the tasks are the same," he said. "Our average boarding population is about 25 mares. We start early, feeding at 7 a.m., picking stalls, exercising and grooming. In between we're cleaning, bedding, medicating and breeding."

The couple is proud of their family business. Their prize stallion, Mr. by Mr., is a world champion, having won the American Quarter Horse Association Reserve Championship in 1996 and the AQHA Congress in 1997. Mr. By Mr.'s offspring, Mr. Cool Cruising is also a champion stallion, winning a Palomino Horse Breeders of America championship in 2000.

"We've won a lot of futurity events," Eddie said, "but those championships are what we are most proud of."

Elisha recalled other wonderful moments associated with their horses. In particular, she remembers Doris Gordon, an elderly lady who fell in love with their prize stallion, Mr. by Mr.

"It was at the AQHA World Congress in Ohio," Elisha said. "All the prize-winning horses were on display and Eddie, Sarah and I were showing Mr. By Mr. to visitors. A sweet lady of almost 80 was enchanted by Mr. She had a bag of chopped apples and carrots, so fed him treats. Mr. seemed to bond with her immediately and they became fast friends. She even gave Mr. a peppermint candy, which led us to call her the Peppermint Lady."

RUNNING A HORSE FARM ISN'T AN EASY VOCATION.

The Peppermint Lady visited Mr. by Mr. and his owners each year at the Congress. She would bring Mr. treats and he would react like a loving child.

"She had treats for us too," Elisha said. "One year she gave us homemade brownies. Mr. would see her coming and recognize her. He would dance, snort and carry on like he remembered her, but he would calm down when she drew close to him. For several years she came to see him. We gave her a Mr. by Mr. stuffed horse, a key chain and some other souvenirs. We even let her sit on him. Mr. is a halter horse so doesn't take riders, but we borrowed a saddle and helped her to mount

<91>

him so her husband could take a picture. One year she called and even asked to speak to Mr. It took forever, but we finally got him to whinny for her."

A year later the Hicks family had Christmas cards made with a picture of themselves posed with Mr. by Mr. They sent the Peppermint Lady a card and in January received a memorable phone call from her husband. He told Elisha that his wife had suffered from short-term memory loss the past year and had to be hospitalized. He had taken the Christmas card to the hospital and when the Peppermint Lady saw it, she smiled and her memory returned.

"She recognized Mr. and the whole family and called them all by name," her husband said, happily.

> "OUR HORSES ARE LIKE LITTLE CHILDREN. THEY DEMAND LOTS OF LOVING CARE, COMPANIONSHIP AND PATIENCE."

"I cried when I got that phone call," Elisha said. "It made me realize how well people can bond with animals and what joy they give us. Our horses are like little children. They demand lots of loving care, companionship and patience. Are they worth it? You can ask the Peppermint Lady. She knows the answer."

Eddie said, "We can all learn patience, kindness and trust from horses, these beautiful members of God's creation. Horses brought Elisha and I together and helped us build a successful business. Our life revolves around our work and our horses, but it's a real labor of love for each of us. It's hard work, but has so many rewards.

"We've met a lot of wonderful people in the process of building this business. We've had breakdowns on the highway and other problems on and off the farm. It seems like there are always caring people to help you along the way."

<93>

THE MAN, THE HORSE

During a fierce Montana blizzard one January night in 1930, an expectant mother was being rushed to the hospital in an open sleigh. The weather was so bad that they had to pull over to the side of the road where she gave birth to her first son.

The first thing the baby boy saw was the back end of the team. Neil Hinck has looked between the ears of horses ever since.

At 5 years of age, he was doing a man's job, mowing and raking the family farm. When Neil turned 8, he discovered he had a knack of training nasty man-killer horses that his ranching neighbors were never able to ride. At 14, he became a jockey, followed by a two-year stint as a top-distance rider.

"I grew up in the Depression when there was no extra money for

< 9 5 >

toys," Neil said. "I was interested in horses, so they were my toys."

His father and grandfather regularly hauled lumber on a 520-mile round trip across the Wyoming and Utah wilderness in the '30s. During that period, young Neil watched how they broke horses and learned from them. He also studied; read everything he could find on the subject and experimented with various techniques. As he got older, he discovered what and didn't work.

"THE HORSE REALIZES THAT YOU'RE A GOOD PERSON THAT YOU'RE A FRIEND."

Now an internationally known teacher, Neil uses a unique system that allows people to train their horses in less than three hours. His Indian rope consists of a small loop that is put over the horse's ears and then under the throat. Depending on how the horse moves, the rope can provide instant relief or a great deal of pressure.

In about 15 minutes using this method, he said people could bond with their horses.

"The horse realizes that you're a good person...that you're a friend," he said. "When the horse runs from you the rope hurts. When he comes to you the pain goes away. You always try to make it easy for the horse to do what you want, rather than what he wants."

With his system, Neil has taught 4-year-old children and 72-year-old adults to train their horses. He said that anyone can learn his method, but a little experience always helps. It is, however, often easier to teach those who have never been exposed to horses, he said, because they do not have preconceived ideas on training or bad habits to overcome.

Horses, Neil said, are still easier to train than their owners.

"Horses have better memories than most humans," he said. "A horse's mind isn't cluttered. A horse doesn't worry about who they're going out with or what they're going to wear. All they worry about is getting a belly full of grain and how they can get out of work if they want to."

Neil said that so far he has never met a horse that he was unable to train. He does not own a whip, he said, because horses feel threatened when they are beaten. He also never tries to train a horse when he is angry.

< 9 6 >

NEIL HINCK

"Horses can read people like they're lit up in neon," he said. "They understand your feelings and the vibes you're sending."

One of his most formidable training challenges was Starburst, an adult zebra, for a Doug Henning World of Magic television special in 1982. Neil soon learned that a zebra can jump over six feet in the air, does not buck like a horse and is unafraid of humans. Undaunted, he gained the zebra's trust quickly and successfully trained Starburst to ride with a saddle and bridle in three weeks.

After the show was over he kept her for 15 years, until her death.

In addition to being a famous trainer, Neil is also known for the innovations that he has introduced to the horse industry. For years he bought and tried hundreds of bits, but felt none of them had been designed with the comfort of the horse in mind. In fact, he said the snaffle bits that are commonly used are vicious and can cause many problems, such as high heads, hollow necks and backs, strung-out bodies and sore mouths. So he designed a bit that frees up the tongue and naturally balances the horse.

Unlike standard bits, Neil's bit has to be tailored to fit in the horse's mouth, just like dentures are designed for people. That factor, along with a lack of time, prevents him from mass-producing his invention. He said that many people have tried to copy his bit, but they "just don't have the eye or knowledge for it."

THEY "JUST DON'T HAVE THE EYE OR KNOWLEDGE FOR IT."

After serving in the military during the Korean War, Neil came home and fulfilled a boyhood dream – developing the Western Blazer horse in the '60s. It took him 30 years to get five horses that suited him, but with these horses he and his wife, Norma, founded the Blazer Horse Association in February of 1967.

By 2000 his herd had grown beyond his wildest dreams – to 1,500 head. His horses can be found in 19 different states, the breed well known for its agility, strength, intelligence and gentleness.

He often sells some of the horses he raises, but not to just anyone who has the money. Neil said he refuses to deal with alcoholics, for example, because they tend to be "inconsistent, awkward and very abusive at times."

His philosophy of dealing with horses is closely connected with

< 9 7 >

the Golden Rule.

"Horses are very much like people," he said. "If you treat them right, most of the time they'll treat you right. Abuse never works. I don't care if it's abuse of your spouse, your children or your pets."

Neil also gives lessons to every person who buys a horse.

"A horse is a one-person animal," he said. "The best-trained horse in the world can be screwed up in a few minutes by the wrong person getting a hold of him."

Because of his many accomplishments people throughout America and Europe seek Neil's advice. They flock to his 30-acre Idaho ranch quite often, and he said it is not unusual for him to see 100 people a day.

"This place is never boring," he said, laughing. "You don't know what's going to happen or who's going to be here. One day when there was a blizzard, no one showed up and the kids thought the world was coming to an end."

> **"IF YOU TREAT THEM RIGHT, MOST OF THE TIME THEY'LL TREAT YOU RIGHT."**

Neil has seven children, 15 grandchildren, and one great-grandchild. His son and six daughters practically grew up on horses. In fact, when his youngest daughter, Sherry, was just three months old, she got plenty of sleep on top of a horse.

"She would sit in front of me on the saddle and be as comfortable as if she was in her bed," he said.

Neil has no intention of retiring any time soon. He wants to continue working as long as he can – though a heart condition limits him to teaching only a few students per day. He still enjoys his interaction with all the people who visit.

"I enjoy teaching people to make dancing partners and buddies out of their horses," he said, "instead of treating them like beasts of burden."

< 9 8 >

<99>

TOMMY HOUSTON

SERIOUS JUDGING

Tommy Houston takes his job as a National Cutting Horse Association (NCHA) judge very seriously. He watches a horse's every move for cleanness and correctness. He looks for that sense of anticipation, grace and ease.

He looks for that glimmer in the horse's eyes, that cock of the ears, that says the animal is intelligent, is thinking."

And every mark he makes on his judging card bears the weight of more than 40 years of riding, owning, training and, above all, loving horses that work.

"The first time I went to the country, when I was just 6 or 7 years old, I knew this is what I wanted to do," said Tommy. "I wanted to be a cowboy."

<101>

Although Tommy's grandfather was a rancher, he spent his early years in Dallas where his father divided his time between the family ranch concerns and his investment business, Standard Investment Company. He first got to know working horses on visits to his grandfather's ranch.

> "THEY DIDN'T WANT ME TO TAKE A HORSE TO SCHOOL, SO I DIDN'T."

At age 15, Tommy was allowed to spend entire summers on the ranch. One of the hands there was an accomplished roper and taught him the art. But he didn't make it easy.

"He told me if I ever got to where I could catch 10 in a row, then I'll really teach you how to rope," said Tommy.

And true to his word, once the budding cowboy was able to catch his 10 consecutive calves, "we proceeded from there to take calf ropin' seriously," said Houston. "And, of course, I was learning a lot about ranching during this time, too."

College, however, threatened to interrupt his cowboy education.

"They didn't want me to take a horse to school [at Texas Tech], so I didn't," he said. "But after I had been there a few weeks, I slipped back here one night, hooked up my trailer and took my horse back to Lubbock with me so I could have something to rope on."

Tommy made the Texas Tech rodeo team and became a professional calf roper, joining the Rodeo Cowboys Association (RCA), now called the Professional Rodeo Cowboys Association (PRCA).

"I had launched my career," he said. "I was a calf roper."

After college, Tommy married and moved back to the family ranch. His father now found himself overburdened with trying to manage the family's ranching operations so, in 1979, he leased part of the ranch to a cutting horse trainer named Buster Welch.

"He was probably one of the most unforgettable people I will ever meet," said Tommy, speaking of the man who was to become his mentor in another equestrian skill – cutting. He refers to Welch as King of the Cutters.

The two men worked out a deal – Welch would give Tommy a cutting horse and teach him how to cut – if he would take some of Welch's rejects and make roping horses out of them.

<102>

And there was sure no danger of running out of horses. Welch was affiliated with the legendary King Ranch of South Texas and had a steady stream of horses through that connection.

"I was taking these King Ranch horses and making ropin' horses out of 'em," said Tommy.

At the same time, under Welch's tutelage, Tommy quickly developed the same love for cutting horses that he had long had for roping horses.

"It became very addictive, both the cutters and the ropers," he said. "The cutters were thinkers. They were athletes, where with the ropers you kind of forced them to do it. The cutters, you kind of tricked 'em into doing it."

Soon Tommy fell naturally into his career as a horse trainer as well as competitor.

"Tio Kleburg [scion of the famous King Ranch family with whom Houston had gone to school] gave me a Mr. San Peppy gelding named San Peppy Chato that didn't make a cutter. They wanted me to train him as a roping horse and show him in calf roping and win the Honor Roll in the AQHA (American Quarter Horse Association). And I not only won the Honor Roll, but at the same time set a record for the most points that had been won on a horse in a single year (1981)."

> "HE'S A CHARACTER. HE'S THE KIND OF A HORSE THAT LIKES TO PLAY."

And the horse did this, Tommy said, despite a name that doesn't exactly befit a champion. "Chato" is Spanish slang for "pugnose."

As a reward Tommy was given San Peppy Chato to keep and he said he has enjoyed the horse more than any he has ever owned.

"He has a lot of personality," he said. "He's a character. He's the kind of a horse that likes to play. Even after being hauled half way across the country for some roping, you would turn him loose in a pen and he would go grab a feed sack and toss and it in the air, let the wind take it and then catch it like a Frisbee. He just loves to play."

Even though Tommy could have sold Pugnose for "tons of money" several times, he refused to part with the versatile pony.

<103>

"I still own the horse," he said. "He's 24-years-old (2000) and he's retired here at the ranch. I think he's probably got about 300 or 400 [AQHA] points because I showed him in the team roping, reining and calf roping."

Some time ago Tommy has shifted his emphasis more toward training cutting horses. He devoted more attention to breeding good horses and one particular mare, Brazos Lynx (out of Sam's Gay Bar by Doc's Lynx), proved to be an outstanding dam.

"All of her colts had done so well, I decided to bite the bullet and breed her to Freckles Playboy, which was a very high stud fee then," said Tommy.

The result of this marriage made in cutting horse heaven, however, was initially a disappointment. He didn't think the new colt, dubbed Freckles Floyd, had much potential.

"I took a look at him and I thought, 'he's just a little bar of soap. I won't even breed the mare back. I'll just let my daughter show her,'" Tommy recalled. "Meanwhile, though, he started to grow and show a lot of personality. I began to show him in some of the biggest shows, and he never won any of them, but he was always in the finals of every major event that year. He was very consistent."

THE RESULT OF THIS MARRIAGE MADE IN CUTTING HORSE HEAVEN, WAS INITIALLY A DISAPPOINTMENT.

Ultimately, Tommy and the "little bar of soap" (Freckles Floyd stands only 14 hands) won the AQHA Honor Roll in cutting. That honor came in 1991, exactly 10 years after Tommy had won the Honor Roll in roping.

"He's our stallion now," he said. "And he is passing his talent along."

Tommy said his first three small crops of colts have already won more than a quarter of a million dollars.

In 1995, Tommy added another skill to his arsenal of horse-related talents. He (born in 1943) took so readily to team roping that he was half of the World Championship team in the senior division in his first year of competing, and repeated that feat in 1996.

Today Tommy somehow finds the time to manage his family's

<104>

pair of ranches in Texas in partnership with his brother, Johnny, and sister, Molly, while continuing to compete in team roping, and remaining active in the cutting world as both a breeder and an NCHA judge. He is also a specialty judge for the AQHA, working calf roping, team roping and cutting events for the association.

"I judge because I've always thought that we owe that to our associations," he said. "We all ought to judge, if we have the ability. It makes you a better cutter."

"I FEEL BLESSED TO BE ABLE TO IDENTIFY GOOD HORSES."

It also makes you a world traveler. Tommy's judging duties have taken him to Canada, Europe and South America.

So having succeeded so impressively in so many areas of horsemanship, what does he find to be the most satisfying aspect of his involvement in horses?

"I feel blessed to be able to identify good horses," Tommy said. "You may go through a 100 head of horses and there might only be one special horse in that bunch. And I've been gifted, or lucky, enough to be able to choose and pursue good horses. I've very seldom had any bad horses. The ones that couldn't be trained didn't last long around here.

Tommy and his wife, Marilyn, have two daughters, Amy Bearden and Emily Barton. The latter daughter is also an avid equestrian who trains and shows horses.

<105>

THE HORSE PROFESSOR

For 14 years, Charlie Hutton taught equine management classes at Ohio State University and the University of Georgia. He enjoyed teaching college students, but he found them hard to read at times. From previous experience, he was sure horses were easier for him to understand.

"If I had one good student in a class of 40, that was pretty good," he said. "When I lectured in front of a class, I couldn't tell who was listening. But when I'm riding, I can always tell if the horse is listening."

At 40 years of age, Charlie decided he preferred training horses to teaching students full-time, so quit his job as a professor. So now the open pens and indoor arenas around his famous 120-acre Hilldale farm in Fayetteville, Tennessee are his classrooms and young Quarter

<107>

Horses are his students.

"The horses never complain, so I like training them better than trying to teach college students," he said.

With family members and assistants, Charlie regularly develops 40 to 50 horses a year into American Quarter Horse Association (AQHA) high-pointers and World Show finalists.

He credits most of his success to his old-fashioned work ethic that gives every horse he meets a chance.

HE QUICKLY DISCOVERED THAT MULES OBEYED SIGNALS RATHER THAN BRUTE FORCE.

"If someone pays you to ride a horse, you put time on him," Charlie said. "Some of the late bloomers that you don't think would be any good in the show ring may turn out to be the best ones."

Working behind draft mules that plowed weeds out of cornrows in the Virginia mountains gave Charlie precious training experience during his boyhood in the '50s. He quickly discovered that mules obeyed signals rather than brute force.

"If there was a big rock in the middle of a row, and you had to step over two lines, you had to redirect them," he said.

During his plowing sessions each day, the youthful Charlie learned to gradually build relationships with the mules that were based on trust and communication.

Nowadays he uses the same system to train his young Quarter Horses for the big shows.

"Horse training boils down to developing a line of communication between two animals that weren't born with a common language, a person and a horse," he said. "It's like being thrown into a room with a person from a little European village who doesn't understood a word of the language you know. The two of you would use hand signals and gradually develop a language."

Communication with a horse for Charlie consists of three stages: ask, tell and demand. The asking part, he said, always comes first.

"Horses are simple, but they have great memories," he said. "You have to show them what you're asking for before you can ask."

After the horse understands what is being asked, Charlie said he

<108>

CHARLIE HUTTON

tells him what to do through positive and negative reinforcement techniques.

"Horses will never come apart if they have enough brains to understand what you're asking," he said, "and if you're doing your job, which is to first show them a road to a reward, and show them what the barriers are if they fail to seek the easy road."

The demand stage, Charlie said, is like "talking to your kid who is sort of listening, but not all that well. So you say, 'Try harder.' And trying harder is what it takes to win at the big shows."

Charlie said he realizes that this process takes time, which suits him fine. He refuses to take shortcuts in training a horse because it ends up taking him months longer to achieve his goals. Instead, he goes to great lengths in developing an understanding between he and the horse.

"I train horses using all the tools I have available," he said. "I teach a horse to obey my voice, my hand, my leg and my seat."

With an elaborate system of signals that only the horse understands, the trainer said he can execute all the quick moves required of cutting horses in the show ring. Charlie takes pride in using imperceptible signals that even judges are unable to notice.

"A dressage master 200 years ago said that a truly light horse obeys the wind from its master's boot," he said. "When the horse feels that you will change direction when you haven't posed your leg because it's still in your mind, that is advanced riding with a great mount."

Charlie thinks that only a few horses he has trained have actually been able to read his mind, though he tries to develop that type of "feel" in all his young horses. But only the great ones actually achieve that level, he said.

The former college professor said Nu Chex to Cash, Hilldale Farm's 1990 palomino stallion, is one that has demonstrated that kind of intuitive ability. He was the 1996 PHBA world champion senior reining and senior working cow horse, and also won the 1999 AQHA high point horse award in those categories.

> "I TEACH A HORSE TO OBEY MY VOICE, MY HAND, MY LEG AND MY SEAT."

<109>

Charlie said his horses have taught him several lessons. He has learned, for example, that a person who rides with excessive emotions, whether fright, anger or anxiety, gets in trouble. Horses, he said, get confused and often change personality if their rider gets in a highly emotional state.

"Suppose a horse thinks he knows the quiet kid who's riding him," he said. "But the kid suddenly gets mad and the horse thinks, 'Who is this person?'"

If parents want to buy a horse for a nervous, uptight child, they should purchase a dull, quiet one, Charlie said.

"On the other hand, if the parents have a quiet, deliberate child, they need to purchase a more active horse for him," he said. "They will get along fine."

Charlie enjoys the challenge of training what he calls "fresh-minded" young horses, because they are like " blackboards that haven't been written on yet."

He said, "Training a willing horse is a thrill for me, no matter how tired I am. I do little things to keep my sanity."

Charlie said he usually starts his day with a nice horse, but one that has a big problem.

"TRAINING A WILLING HORSE IS A THRILL FOR ME, NO MATTER HOW TIRED I AM. I DO LITTLE THINGS TO KEEP MY SANITY."

"Because I'm fresh, know what the problem is and have had time to think about it, I'm better prepared to handle it," he said. "I always finish my day with a horse that has a good mind and who will let me make him a little better than he was yesterday. Then I can go back to the house feeling better about both myself and my horses."

Charlie said every family member shares his love for horses. Tammye, his wife, shows frequently. In 2000 she was the primary exhibitor of Nu Fancee Cash, a leading national contender in both the reining and cow horse classes. She also showed Zans Red Gold to win two of her three consecutive Honor Roll cow horse titles.

The couple's daughter, Sarah Locker, born in 1989, won the 1997 AQHA high point award with her halter mare. She now plans to

<110>

get a scholarship after high school and become a veterinarian.

Daughter Jessicah Keller, born in 1985, has been awarded many high-point rankings with working cow horses and reining horses. She wants to follow in her father's footsteps by becoming a horse trainer.

Son David already trains horses with his father and won the national high point title in AQHA youth reining at age 14. Now, he specializes in starting 2 year olds and training these and older horses on cattle.

"Showing horses has been a benefit to our whole family," Charlie said. "It gives our children the chance to be around adults more, which in turn gives them more respect for us. They also have learned to set goals and work toward them."

> "SHOWING HORSES HAS BEEN A BENEFIT TO OUR WHOLE FAMILY."

<111>

ast Coast Amateur
CHAMPIONSHIP SHOW 1997
EAST COAST AMATEUR CHAMPIONSHIP SHOW
19 VA 97
1997
CIRCUIT
CHAMPION
DonTrout ©

A BROTHER ACT

As a boy growing up in Virginia during the '60s, Mike Jennings was always intrigued by the television commercial in which the auctioneer cried, "Sold American." Fascinated that "anyone could talk that fast," the young Mike spent hours listening to The Auctioneers Song by Leroy Van Dyke.

Mike's father, who was the president of the Virginia Quarter Horse Association in 1969, developed his interest further by taking him along with his other two brothers, Tim and Steve, to horse auctions all over the state.

"Anytime anybody said the word 'auction,' we were ready to go," Mike said laughing.

All three brothers loved horses and won many competitions dur-

<113>

ing their teenage years.

Mike, the oldest, won State 4-H championships and was high point youth all-around in the Virginia Quarter Horse Association on his favorite horse, Chance's Pride. In 1987, he was the National Reining Horse Association Reserve World Champion in Limited Non-Pro Reining.

"WE HAVE A GREAT APPRECIA- TION FOR GOD'S CREATION AND HOW SPECIAL THESE HORSES ARE."

Tim, the middle brother, showed Chance's Pride and won the reserve high-point youth award for the state.

Steve, the youngest, earned awards in open shows and enjoyed recreational riding. He earned a master's degree in equine reproduction.

"We have a great appreciation for God's creation and how special these horses are," Tim said. "It's a shared family passion."

During Mike's senior year of high school, several people began to approach his father to manage auctions for them to disperse their horses. The first involved two different dispersal and production sales of horses owned by radio and television celebrity Arthur Godfrey.

Mike attended Virginia Tech for two years and then came home to do "horse stuff," which included standing several AQHA champion stallions during the early '70s. He became more involved in auction management and graduated from the Superior School of Auctioneering in 1971.

Tim also caught the auction fever and graduated from the same school in 1976, leading to the brothers forming their own company, Professional Auction Services, Inc., in 1978. Since its inception, the corporation has managed more than 160 horse auctions in seven states with gross sales of nearly $70 million.

In 1995, Professional Auction Services was chosen by the American Quarter Horse Association (AQHA) to hold the prestigious AQHA World Championship Quarter Horse Show Sale. The company's flagship sale, however, is the highly regarded Eastern Mid-Winter Sale, which draws approximately 7,000 people each year in late January.

Professional Auction Services also proudly supports youth schol-

<114>

arships through the American Quarter Horse Foundation.

Mike, Tim and Steve all have different roles in the company. Mike takes on the majority of the actual auctioneer duties and also serves as the manager of the Equine Sales Division. Tim handles the advertising and marketing aspects of the business, as well as selecting horses for the auctions. Steve deals with all the logistics involved with the auctions, such as production, set up and staffing.

"Our personalities are different, which creates a very good balance," Tim said. "At meetings we share various viewpoints and, generally, we've been pretty successful with what we've come up with."

The Jennings brothers cater to a "broad spectrum of the Quarter Horse and Paint horse industry." People who attend their auctions range from pet quality owners to world show competitors. Yet, the brothers like to create an informal, family atmosphere that makes everyone comfortable. In fact, many people come to their auctions to socialize and end up buying horses that they liked.

"If our customers were regular buyers in a strictly commercial setting and didn't want other dealers to know they were bidding on a horse, they would set up little signals with us," Mike said. "But that's not the type of customers we deal with. Our people are like those who go to the estate or antique auctions."

Mike and Tim also moderate the pace of their faster livestock auction chant for the benefit of the crowds.

"We have to be understood, because of our clientele," Mike said. "We make sure we stop and slow down, and let people know where we are, because if they're confused, they won't bid."

From his vantage as an auctioneer, Mike observes a whole gamut of emotion, from excitement about selling a horse for thousands of dollars to disappointment that a horse is not worth as much as previously thought.

> MANY PEOPLE COME TO THEIR AUCTIONS TO SOCIALIZE AND END UP BUYING HORSES THAT THEY LIKED.

"Sitting in an auction box and watching people make their decisions about the horses is a lot of fun," he said. "You see the stress they put themselves under and the joy they have when they get one

<115>

bought."

Sometimes people have trouble parting with their horses, but they are afraid to show their emotions. Mike said that he also has seen a lot of tears shed behind the auction box, because some individuals are sad about selling their horse.

An emotional experience for Mike happened during the 75th Annual Chincoteague Pony auction that the company hosted in August of 2000. Legend has it that during the 1700s Spanish galleons loaded with ponies wrecked off the coast near Chincoteague, a tiny island off the eastern end of Virginia. The horses swam to shore and survived in the wild.

In the early 1900s the local fire department sold some of the ponies as a fund-raiser. This started the tradition of the annual pony swim and auction, an event that has become internationally famous. For conservation purposes only the foals are sold – and they often fetch high prices.

During the auction children and adults buy the ponies for an average price of $2,000 each. Some people, Mike said, buy them just to have a piece of the legend.

> MIKE SAID THAT HE ALSO HAS SEEN A LOT OF TEARS SHED BEHIND THE AUCTION BOX.

"A reporter asked what it meant to me to do this auction and I got choked up," Mike said. "Growing up as a horse-crazy kid in Virginia, I knew all about the legend of Chincoteague. It was amazing to be involved in that."

Other than being an auctioneer, Mike is also an AQHA – approved judge in his 20th year of service, having officiated at the AQHA Youth World Championship three times. Now, however, he has cut back on judging competitions so he can enjoy more time with his family and attend the Methodist church in Round Hill, but he currently serves as national director from Virginia for the AQHA.

"Both my wife's family and mine were active in church when we were younger," Mike said. "Our part of the horse business revolves around our customers' hobby time, which is on weekends. It was not that we felt any different about our faith, but we were always going somewhere on weekends. We got back into church a lot more because

<116>

we wanted our kids to have that as a part of their foundation when it comes time for them to make important decisions."

Mike's wife, Stephanie, their daughter, Kendall (born in 1988) and son, Tyler (born in 1991) compete in horse competitions. Stephanie showed a World Champion Limited Non-Pro Reiner in the NRHA in 1987. Kendall, who also enjoys playing soccer, competes in the basic western pleasure riding classes. Tyler, a drama student, likes the costume class.

Tim, his wife, Cathy, and son, Travis (born 1990), also enjoy competing in the top end of Quarter Horse competition. Tim won the amateur western riding event at the Quarter Horse Congress in Ohio, the largest single breed horse show in the world. In 1989, Held Captive, owned by Cathy, became the first horse ever to win all three divisions of the Congress Hunter Under Saddle Futurity. He won approximately $30,000 in prizes and awards.

> "OVER THE YEARS, WE'VE SEEN HOW HORSES CAN BE GOOD FOR YOUNG PEOPLE."

Travis has earned two AQHA Youth Superior Halter awards, and in 1999 ranked 5th nationally in the AQHA (11 and under) Rookie division. Tim currently serves on the executive board of the National Snaffle Bit Association. The family attends the Methodist church in Summit Point, Virginia.

"Over the years, we've seen how horses can be good for young people," Mike said. "Because of their interest in horses, it gives them a purpose. They can get a horse to do something for them-whether it's doing a fast spin, cutting a cow, jumping a big fence, or galloping across a pasture. If young people can ever feel that good, they wouldn't do drugs at all."

<117>

BOB & ANNE KEEN

STRAIGHT TALK

From his earliest days Bob Keen has had two passions: horses and the law. At the ripe age of 5, he was scheming about how to escape the cold, hard life of the coal mines in his native Keen Mountain, Virginia. He and a young cousin conspired to escape to Oklahoma, where she would be a waitress and he would find work as a cowboy and small-town sheriff.

But it was the Navy that would ship Bob to sunnier waters. He enlisted in 1952, choosing the Navy because "they had the best uniforms." His tour carried him as far as Hong Kong, Australia and Tokyo before he returned to the States and settled in North Carolina — where his mother, Ester, had relocated — and he quickly picked up where he had left off on his cowboy/sheriff dreams.

<119>

In 1955, he established Circle K Ranch in Burlington, North Carolina. The bright red four-stall barn was the backdrop for gaming classes and match races. Bob began to learn the horse training ropes from several professionals.

It was a good start, but not everything he had dreamed. He still wasn't sheriff, and cash flow was a little tight in those early years. So he turned to the law.

> **"IF YOU WANT SOME-ONE WHO CAN PUT'M IN JAIL, I'M YOUR GUY."**

He tried to hire on with the Burlington Police Department, but Chief Jesse James, who was physically challenged with a wooden leg, didn't want to hire someone with a speech impediment. Bob has never considered his stuttering as a disability. It's actually an "extra thinking time advantage," he said.

"If you want somebody to talk'm into jail, I'm not the one," Bob told the sheriff, "but if you want someone who can put'm in jail, I'm your guy."

He was hired on the spot.

Bob graduated from the New York Institute of Criminology and during his 30 years of service rose to the rank of lieutenant. He gained a reputation for his intolerance of the abuse of children, the elderly and alcohol – as well as his compassion for those in need. On more than one occasion he gave his last dollar to a family he thought needed groceries or oil for their heater, said his wife, Anne.

Back at the ranch, Bob was working overtime. He was leading something of a double life: lawman by day, horseman by night. And he loved every minute of it.

In 1960, Bob bought Bart's Lucky Moon, who showed well both in halter and western pleasure.

"Keep in mind that this was a period when a halter horse was also a riding horse," he said. Bart's Lucky Moon would be the first of several point earning halter and pleasure horses for Bob.

That same year, with help from his mother, he bought 50 acres in Graham, North Carolina, and he, his mom and the Circle K relocated. He began training horses for others, often working eight- to 12-hour shifts for the local police department before coming home and riding late into the night to make sure all the horses were getting the

<120>

attention needed.

As Bob sees it: "If you take someone's money for training, you need to ride the horse every day, five to six days a week. Rain or shine, cold or hot."

In 1972, Bob married for the first time and the couple soon had a son, Robert Ellis Keen Jr. Over the years Bob would say that his son's passion for horses was second only to his enthusiasm for motorcycles.

Father and son worked on the ranch side by side for many years and the Circle K's breeding program thrived in the '80s with the acquisition of Royal Scooter Bar and Noveto Riker. But late in that decade, when his son left for college and he retired his badge, the Circle K sold its breeding stallions and Bob turned his focus to his one unfulfilled dream: becoming sheriff.

"Bob does not and never has viewed the position of sheriff as a job of punishing people," Anne said. "He has always talked about it as an opportunity to help people, especially the old and less fortunate."

Bob hit the political trail with his eyes on the sheriff's post in Alamance County. Not even his stuttering slowed him down.

"Even during the numerous speeches that are required when running for public office, he never once hesitated or questioned his own abilities," Anne said.

But it wasn't enough. Bob lost the 1986 election by a nose and returned full time to horse training, and Circle K began specializing in breaking and training 2-year olds.

Calamity soon followed. Bob and his first wife divorced a few years later. And in 1995, misfortune struck again, when he crushed his shoulder in a training accident. He had to hire a trainer to keep the business going.

"BOB DOES NOT AND NEVER HAS VIEWED THE POSITION OF SHERIFF AS A JOB OF PUNISHING PEOPLE."

But Bob's outlook soon took a brighter turn. In the late 1990s, he met Anne Melvin, a critical care heart nurse with a passion for thoroughbreds. Together they breathed new life into the Circle K.

They began hand selecting brood mares and scouring the South for a world-class stallion. They found – and fell in love with – Zpine,

<121>

the son of the legendary Zippo Pine Bar, in Lexington, Virginia.

Zpine was soon sent to Ohio for training, while the pair searched for Congress/World level trainers. In late '98/early '99, Jeff Hall of North Carolina and his wife, Renee Hall of New York, were tapped to spearhead Circle K's new training program. Anne Randle, a vet tech from Florida, came on board to steer the breeding program.

But Bob's collision with tragedy wasn't over. In February – the beginning of the breeding season – Zpine died during colic surgery.

"With the entire farm in shock, a full book of mares to breed, we made phone calls, got on a plane and traveled all over the southeastern United States for one week solid before finding the perfect stallion to replace Zpine," Anne recalled.

That same month, Circle K bought Classic Mac Goodbar, a black bay, 16-hand stallion by the great Zippos Mr. Good Bar from Richland Ranch in Illinois.

"With a diligent advertising campaign and the help of a lot of people in the horse business, Mac stood to a full book his first year of breeding," Anne said.

MAC STOOD TO A FULL BOOK HIS FIRST YEAR OF BREEDING.

And 1999 ended on a very happy note: On Christmas Eve, Bob and Anne were married at the Circle K.

The Keens' Circle K Ranch now is home to some 40 horses, six breeding stallions and 13 brood mares. It houses a 25-stall barn, a competition-size ring, two training rings and a 10-stall stallion barn, with plans for another 20-stall barn with an indoor show ring.

"We own some of the top bloodlines in the county, consisting of Zips' Chocolate Chip, Sweet Talkin Chip, Zippos Mr. Good Bar, Radical Rodder, Good Version, Kid Clue and a thoroughbred stallion Grand Hoorah and own son of Rahy," Anne noted.

She said the ranch's present operation is threefold:

• breeding quarter and thoroughbred horses for English hunt seat, halter and western pleasure;

• serving as a private coaching and training facility focusing on Novice, Youth AQHA showing at the World and Congress levels;

• providing a full-service breeding operation, including shipped

<122>

semen, semen analysis, mare insemination and pregnancy detection by Ultrasound.

"We both wanted more – for the ranch to be the best it could be," Anne said. "We chose western pleasure and halter due to Bob's knowledge and hunter under saddle because of my experience with thorough-breds. Like everyone who enters a business venture, we just want to be the best at what we do."

And as for Bob's aspirations to be sheriff, there's another election around the corner.

Born in 1934, Bob said his mother and Uncle Elbert Hess (who helped raise him) were the greatest influences in his life. He lost both of them in 1998, but the values they instilled in him will never die.

A clock Bob gave to his uncle hangs in the office at the ranch. It says: "To Ebb Hess, who taught me the values of hard work, dedication and honesty. These are the values the Circle K Ranch was built on."

"WE BOTH WANTED MORE – FOR THE RANCH TO BE THE BEST IT COULD BE."

< 1 2 3 >

LIVING A DREAM

Bill and Ann Lanning have long been involved with horses. It was this interest that brought the two of them together as teenagers and their love for each other and horses have been intertwined ever since.

Their dedication to the horse business brought them to Edgewood Farms in Pilot Point, Texas. For 18 years the couple managed Edgewood Farms, helping to make it one of the premier Quarter Horse ranches in the nation. The ranch was later sold and the Lannings made the decision in 1997 to purchase land and build a new ranch of their own. They now own and operate a facility for breeding and training just down the road from their former location in Pilot Point.

<125>

"We usually have about 150 horses on the ranch as we keep a lot of customer horses on a year round basis," Ann said. "We specialize in the halter horse end of the business, but also stand performance stallions to the public in addition to the halter stallions."

> "A WINNING HORSE HAS TO BE PERFECTLY BALANCED FROM ITS HEAD TO ITS TAIL."

"Halter horses are the body builders of the breed," Bill said. "They're judged on their looks and conformation. A winning horse should be balanced...a model of what you would like to see in the perfect horse. I can take a look at a horse and just know that with the right kind of feed and work it could be a world champion. A winning horse has to be perfectly balanced from its head to its tail."

"You want a horse that's real straight legged and strong across the top of its back, a halter horse must be your perfect horse," Ann added. "To accomplish that requires a lot of work for me, Bill and the horse."

The Lannings have developed a workout program specifically designed to sculpture and condition a horse to the point where it is blue ribbon perfect. Bill and Ann look at these horses as if they were Olympic caliber athletes. First they ease them into shape and then, under careful supervision, each horse is given an exercise program specifically designed to maximize its physical development.

"Our work and exercise program is specifically designed for each individual horse's needs," Ann said. "Where we start with that program depends on the horse's physical condition and age...and we make sure the horse is fit from the inside out with a good worm and health regiment plus nutritious feed. Grooming also plays a big part in the preparation of the horse for the show ring and time is allocated each day for every horse to be cleaned, brushed and rubbed on to keep a glossy shine on their coats."

Bill said that although not every horse has what it takes to be a world champion, each animal can be improved upon thus giving it an opportunity to reach it's maximum potential.

"We strive to give every horse a chance to be the best they can be," he said. "We work six days a week to get these horses into championship shape. We start our horses off on the pony track for 15 to 20

<126>

minutes a day. Then we get them on a long trot which is the best way to build muscle mass for the entire body."

After all that preparation the horse is ready to put his or her best hoof forward and, according to Bill and Ann, the horses are mentally and physically ready to strut their stuff for the judges.

"When we lead our horses into the pen they pick up on the excitement and they know its show time," said Ann. "They definitely know they're being judged and many times we've seen that winning attitude reflected in their expression and demeanor."

Bill said horses, like human athletes, cannot stay in peak condition all the time. He said there's a time to work and a time to play, and that a blending of the two creates a horse with a winning look and personality.

"For example," he said, "when we train a horse for the Congress and it does well, then it may go to the World Show. That's similar to a track star training for two big races in a row. When an event is over a track star may need some time to rest mentally and physically before the next one. Horses may need to relax after a big event, too. So we take them off the work program for a while and let them be regular horses again and have some fun."

Bill and Ann have been associated with some of the best show and breeding horses in the Quarter Horse industry, the most famous being the AQHA stallion, Mr. Conclusion.

> HORSES, LIKE HUMAN ATHLETES, CANNOT STAY IN PEAK CONDITION ALL THE TIME.

Mr. Conclusion came into their care as a 2-year-old when he was purchased by Edgewood Farms, Inc., and thus began a relationship with a horse that would not only be special to those closest to him but to the entire Quarter horse breed.

For 12 years Bill and Ann shared in Mr.'C's daily life. And during this time he rose to greatness. They watched proudly as Mr. Conclusion was crowned a World Champion Halter Stallion and as he went on to become "The All Time Leading Sire of AQHA & AQHYA World and Reserve World Champions," with 216 titles to his credit. Mr. Conclusion retains a sire record that has never before been equaled and probably never will be again.

<127>

"That is a remarkable accomplishment when you stop and consider that there are now nearly 4,000,000 horses registered with AQHA around the world," Ann said.

In August of 1996, Mr. Conclusion was sold by Edgewood Farms and moved to Florida, but the big stallion never left the hearts of Bill and Ann. In October 1998, at age 16, Mr. Conclusion was put to sleep after developing laminitis. He was buried in Florida.

Although Bill and Ann were not afforded the opportunity to tell their friend farewell, they said there is some comfort for them in knowing that he was laid to rest with his head facing west towards Texas.

"Mr. Conclusion was the best and still is the best," says Bill emphatically. "People would come from all around the world just to see him in person. He was a true celebrity and he loved his fans. Mr. Conclusion was a real people horse and we miss him a lot."

The Lannings raised and own a World Champion son of Mr. Conclusion that is making his own way as a sire. His name is Conclusified and they are very excited over his offspring and what the future holds for him.

Avid animal lovers, Bill and Ann have dedicated their lives to the horses that call their ranch home.

"WE LOVE WHAT WE DO AND OUR ANIMALS HAVE BECOME OUR FAMILY AND CHILDREN."

"We love what we do and our animals have become our family and children; the horses, the dogs and the lion," Ann said.

Yes, that's correct, she said lion. Since 1987 they have been the proud parents of an African lioness named Elsa.

"We acquired her when she was only 7 days old and she became a very big part of our life from that day on," Ann said. "She lived in the house with us and slept in our bed until she was around 225 pounds. Bill felt she was taking up too much of the king size bed and preparation was begun to make her a house of her own in the back yard. When we decided to build the new ranch, Elsa was the first one to take up residence there."

Today Elsa weighs in at about 375 pounds and thoroughly enjoys her own special place on the ranch; just behind the show barn and

<128>

BILL & ANNE LANNING

complete with her own swimming pool.

"Elsa thinks we're her parents," said Ann. "She runs loose and goes everywhere with us. She has never hurt a soul. In fact, Elsa loves to play with our dogs and wrestle with Bill. She's very friendly and we just love her to death."

From training and raising world class Quarter Horses to being the parents to a giant pussycat, Bill and Ann Lanning are living a dream come true. For this happy couple, true bliss comes from a job well done and the love of the animals with which they share their success.

> "ELSA LOVES TO PLAY WITH OUR DOGS AND WRESTLE WITH BILL."

<129>

BREAD AND BUTTER

Webster's Dictionary defines the word synergy as a combined or cooperative action or force. Nowhere is such action better demonstrated than in the story of Bob and Nina Lundgren, a husband and wife team whose union of spirit produces extraordinary achievements in the ranching world.

Born and raised on opposite sides of the Rocky Mountains, even their names were melted together to identify their farming and ranching enterprise. From Bob and Nina they forged Bonina, a name that has come to illustrate how great accomplishments are born when hearts and minds are synchronized.

Colorado was Bob's home, where he learned farming and graduated from the prestigious Colorado State University Veterinary

< 1 3 1 >

School, which has consistently been ranked among the top veterinary schools in the country. He gained experience practicing large animal medicine in Colorado, Idaho and Nevada. He then focused his talents on ranch and feed lot management, consulting for the JR Simplot company and others.

"WE PIC-NICKED AMONG A HERD OF CATTLE THAT BOB WAS FEED-ING ON TURNIPS."

Bob managed several cattle ranches, including the 2,000,000-acre, 15,000 head, Nevada-Garvey ranch. Bob was later hired as manager for the 50,000 head McGregor Feed lot in Pasco, Washington. He eventually bought the feed lot, converted it to a custom cattle-feeding facility and then sold it to Simplot Cattle Feeders.

Nina was raised in the high desert country of central Oregon. She had her first horse at the age of 10 and wasted no time mastering the equestrian arts. Horses, cattle, ranch work, and junior rodeos were her youthful life's focus. She graduated from Cal Polytechnic College, San Luis Obispo, majoring in Animal Husbandry, an environment where livestock judging, colt training, cattle showing and feeding trials gave her a foundation for the future. Her life has been an extension of that foundation – breeding, promoting and selling great cattle and competitively riding superb horses.

Bob and Nina met while Bob was in feed lot management. Nina was then a veterinary pharmaceutical representative for American Cyanamid Corporation. She often-made business calls to Bob's location and before long their work association blossomed into a more serious personal relationship.

Nina remembers their unusual first date.

"It was on a New Year's Day holiday," she recalled. "We picnicked among a herd of cattle that Bob was feeding on turnips."

That same blending of work and social activity became the foundation for the couple's eventual merger as business partners, best friends and husband and wife. Each brought different attributes to their union.

"Nina is outgoing, social, active and extroverted," Bob said. "She gets things started, whereas I tend to be more introverted and conservative."

The combination has proved successful. It began in earnest when

<132>

they established the Bonina Ranch near Eltopia in eastern Washington, 15 miles north of Pasco. Here and at another facility in Mesa, Washington, they have developed multifaceted farm and ranch operations. They raise registered Simmental, Angus and Braunvieh cattle, breed and raise Jack Russell Terriers and also breed Quarter horses.

Bob is heavily involved in feeding cattle and farming, which includes raising alfalfa hay, corn and asparagus, but at the ranch, he is also regularly called upon to practice his training as a veterinarian.

Nina oversees the calving, artificial insemination, embryo transfer and training of the horses and the marketing of cattle, horses and puppies.

"We work as a team and take great pride in the care, selection and production of our animals," she said.

Nina is particularly proud of their Quarter Horses.

"We raise beautiful working specimens," she said. "Our black stallion, Hesa Onyx Gem, consistently stamps his colts with beautiful heads, perfectly straight legs, well muscled rumps, good dispositions and lots of ability."

Nina's pride is well founded. The Lundgrens have earned an American Quarter Horse Association (AQHA) Award, recognising 10 years of breeding success.

Yet Bob and Nina have not limited their venture to breeding show horses. Both have spent their lives in the livestock industry and recognize the kind of cattle and horses that ranchers want.

"We are squarely on both sides of the cattle and horse business," Nina said. "Our bread and butter is producing range bulls, but we get a thrill from receiving a thank you and a win picture from a customer who has just taken Grand Champion with a Bonina bred bull or heifer. Likewise, we have raised and sold good solid ranch horses for several years, but have also discovered the thrill of riding cutting horses. Our horse business has now expanded to encompass the best of all equine athletes, cow cutters."

Riding merits run high for the Lundgrens. Nina has won several saddle championships and Bob rides in similar competitions. Bob and Nina usually compete in both the Northwest Cutting Horse

> "OUR BREAD AND BUTTER IS PRODUCING RANGE BULLS."

<133>

Association (NWCHA) and the Washington Cutting Horse Association (WCHA).

"The sport and the competition are addictive," Nina said. "There is nothing greater than the thrill of a 76 and nothing more humbling than losing a cow. We are fortunate to be well mounted. I'm riding Dirty Dually and Amandas Foxy Dually. They helped me win five saddles in 1999. Dirty has packed me through the learning phases to some thrilling wins. In 2000, we won Reserve Champion in the Non Pro and won the $50,000 Amateur Class. And we won the Non Pro Championship and the $10,000 Novice Non Pro in the WCHA.

Bob rides a son of Dual Pep known as Uncle Vic.

"He is the cutest, quickest little horse (13.3 hands) on the circuit," Nina said. "He is so cow smart and turns so quickly that he has been a challenge to ride. With Bob's determination, he and Uncle Vic won the $10,000 Amateur in Washington Cutting Horse Association competitions."

Bob also showed a gorgeous grey mare named Buck's Little Orphan to the Reserve Championship in the $3,000 Novice Non Pro in the WCHA. He and Buck's Little Orphan won the Washington Classic/Challenge for 5-6 year olds in June 2000.

"THE SPORT AND THE COMPETITION ARE ADDICTIVE."

Despite the endless tasks associated with managing Bonina and riding competitively, Bob and Nina enjoy a lot of variety in their lives.

"We seem to be a magnet for young people," she said. "We enjoy our children, grandchildren and other family members who live nearby. We are grooming our grandchildren in the care and enjoyment of all our animals and are introducing them to riding as well. We also enjoy the many friends who join us for dinner...often late at night after the work or the riding is done. We have also tried to help a lot of people. We encourage young folks to go on to school and better themselves."

The Lundgrens sum up their philosophy of life and reason for success in a favorite quote of author James Michener:

"The Master in the art of living makes little distinction between his work and his play, his labor and his leisure, his mind and his body, his information and his recreation, his love and his religion. He hardly

<134>

knows which is which. He simply pursues his vision of excellence whatever he does, leaving it to others to decide whether he is working or playing. To him, he is always doing both."

For the Lundgrens, their work, their play and their synergy have become a gentle harmony of two people working as one – to attain composite dreams.

> "HE SIMPLY PURSUES HIS VISION OF EXCELLENCE WHATEVER HE DOES."

<135>

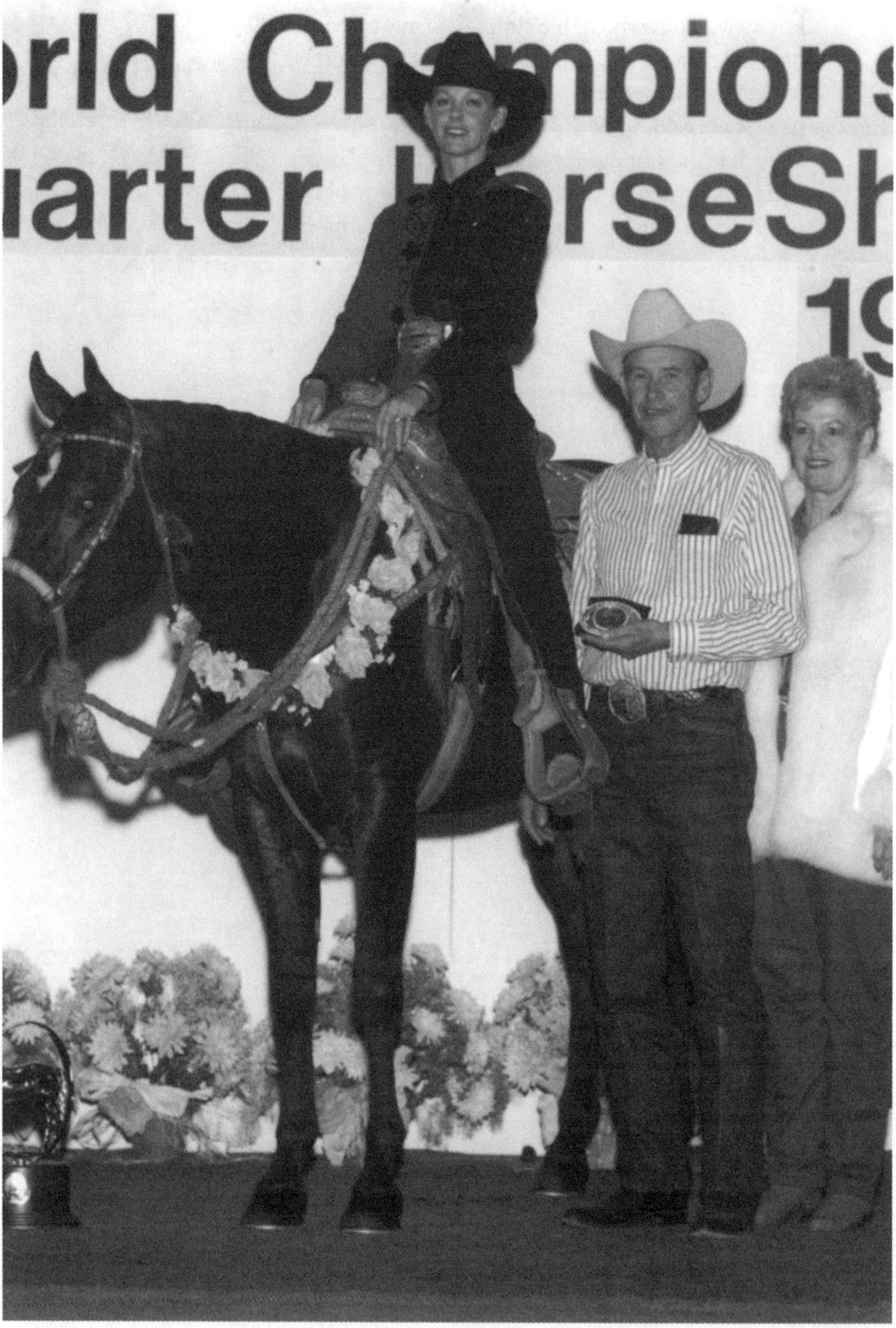
orld Champions
uarter HorseSh
19

FIELD OF DREAMS

Brad and Kelli McCamy have their own "Field of Dreams," along with a ranch near Allen and Plano, Texas where they engage in three of their great loves – breeding, training and showing horses.

The couple built the baseball field (their Field of Dreams) behind the barn to save some of Brad's time. He helps coach the team for which their 13-year-old son, Wesley, plays.

"Brad is big time into baseball," Kelli said, "so we have a field behind the barn and a batting cage in our arena. We can raise it to the top when not in use. All the kids seem to like having their own special field."

Kelli, who was born in Kermit, Texas, said she didn't exactly get off on the right foot (or hoof) with horses.

< 1 3 7 >

"My dad was in the oil business, so my parents lived in a lot of little towns in West Texas," she said. "But when I was 2 years old, they settled in Hobbs, New Mexico. And since dad was raised on a farm and loved horses, I was around them from the time I was a baby. In dad's spare time we would go out into the country and ride horses, but when I was 4 or 5 years old I was thrown and didn't want to have anything to do with them."

> "WHEN I WAS 4 OR 5 YEARS OLD I WAS THROWN AND DIDN'T WANT TO HAVE ANYTHING TO DO WITH THEM."

Kelli said that changed when she was 10 or 11 years old.

"I asked my parents to buy me a horse and they got me a quarter horse," she said. "I took 10 lessons and then started riding on my own. Dad had a real interest in horses so encouraged me and bought a couple more. So every day after school I went to the barns to ride and work with the horses."

And she started showing horses, traveling to distant sites with her parents.

"We moved to Dallas when I was 12," Kelli said, "and that put me into an even larger culture of people who breed, train and show horses. I had already witnessed the commitment and intense competitiveness of people in the business, but all that was magnified in a metropolitan area like Dallas."

Brad, on the other hand, grew up northwest of Houston in Bellville.

"He grew up in the country and has loved horses all his life," Kelli said. "When he was a kid his family couldn't afford to buy him a horse, so he worked summers, after school and on weekends to earn enough money to buy one. He learned everything he could about horses and started showing when he was a teenager."

The couple went to Texas A&M University, where Kelli majored in agriculture journalism, but they didn't meet until later – during a period when Kelli was working in the public relations department for the Texas Quarter Horse Association. They married in '84 and Kelli joined Brad in the horse breeding business he had established in Brenham, Texas.

< 1 3 8 >

BRAD & KELLI MCCAMY

"I never really anticipated being in the horse business, except as a hobby," Kelli said. "After getting my degree from Texas A&M, I figured I would do something in journalism."

Kelli's parents had bought land in the Allen-Plano area before she went to college, and offered it to the couple if they wanted to bring their horse training business to North Texas.

"So we set up business here and over the years have just kept building," Kelli said. "And I'm so happy with what we do that I can't imagine doing anything else."

The McCamys have two main barns, one of which is for brood mares and babies. It has 20 stalls inside and 10 outside. There is also a show barn, which has 18 stalls, plus a riding arena. All of this is on 78 acres.

"Most of the time we have around 75 horses here," Kelli said, "but during breeding season we may have as many as 150."

As for building a successful breeding business, Kelli admitted it was tough, and she attributed the success they have enjoyed to their stallion, Impulsions, which won the 2-Year-Old Snaffle Bit Western Pleasure World Championship in '89. And Impulsions was All-American Quarter Horse Congress Champion in the 3-Year-Old Western Pleasure Derby in '90.

"He built our breeding business," Kelli said. "He's the reason we get mares from all over the country.

"HE'S THE REASON WE GET MARES FROM ALL OVER THE COUNTRY."

"We still train and show horses," she said, "but making a living training horses, and all the hoopla and limelight associated with it, requires a lot of work and travel. And it's a very expensive hobby if it's not done professionally.

"I want to make it clear that we began with a training business, but have been blessed with a successful breeding business after being successful with Impulsions as a show horse.

Kelli said she and Brad take a lot of pride in a self-owned business, and that their employees (at least four and sometimes more) love the horses as much as they do.

"If you didn't love it, getting up and starting work at six o'clock

<139>

in the morning and checking the barns at nine or 10 o'clock at night before going to bed would get awfully old," she said. "I won't deny that it's a tough way to make a living, and we're very blessed that Impulsions came along because he made it possible for us not to have to be on the road all the time.

"The world championship Impulsions won is special, but the most special part of it has to do with the fact that I love horses. And the people who go along with the horses we train are special. So business blossoms into friendship, because people who own horses usually find they have a lot of other things in common."

Kelli said the business she and Brad are in provides a unique position to meet people.

"People from all over this nation, and Canada, send their kids to live with us in the summer," she said. "We take pride in the fact that we're trusted to mentor them. And there's no way I could have ever dreamed that we would be in such a position, but I'm grateful that this business enables us to reinforce a deep sense of values and ethics in kids.

Kelli said some 12- and 13-year olds that they have taught are now grown and coming back with their kids.

"This thing with horses, it's pretty addictive," she said. "We have to teach kids that their horse isn't a pet. You can't trust them too much. You have to respect them, and you have to make them respect you.

> **"PEOPLE FROM ALL OVER THIS NATION, AND CANADA, SEND THEIR KIDS TO LIVE WITH US."**

"Our son, Wesley, had a horse that he fed hamburgers. He has fun with all his horses, and we let the kids have fun, but you have to factor in that respect."

Kelli related the story of a kid who had no interest in anything other than video games, but after his sister started taking riding lessons he began showing an interest in horses.

"Before long he was here every morning about eight o'clock and he stayed until five in the afternoon," she said. "His parents hadn't been able to get him to focus on anything, but now he's eaten up with horses.

BRAD & KELLI MCCAMY

"The truth is, before I got into showing horses I was very shy. But showing in front of thousands of people changes your entire personality. I think there are a million a one benefits to being involved with horses, and tremendous pleasure."

Kelli said she loves cooking and working with kids, and that she and Brad are also active in First Baptist Church at Allen.

"All of our time is juggled between church activities, baseball games, our business and, hopefully, a little time we try to reserve for a family vacation when we can," she said.

> "SHOWING IN FRONT OF THOUSANDS OF PEOPLE CHANGES YOUR ENTIRE PERSONALITY."

< 1 4 1 >

BRENT MCCULLAR

A HORSEMAN
WITH DRIVE

Customers walking into Brent McCullar's office know immediately that his passion is horses. Horse memorabilia covers each wall, including a photograph of a Skipper W stud and a painting of a mare and her colt. On his desk a porcelain music box plays the theme from the Bonanza television series.

By day Brent operates a GMC/Oldsmobile automobile dealership in Rector, Arkansas. And because he sells trucks, he deals with plenty of horse owners who need them to pull their trailers.

"Those guys kid me all the time about me having horses on the brain," Brent said, laughing.

When Brent leaves the auto dealership at day's end, he drives 20 miles south to his elegant colonial-style plantation home in the rolling

< 1 4 3 >

hills just outside Paragould. His place is far enough out in the country that sometimes he can see deer eating fruit off the apple and peach trees in the backyard.

He said that after a stressful day at the dealership, working with his horses in the evening is a relaxing change of pace.

BRENT'S LOVE FOR HORSES GOES BACK TO HIS CHILD-HOOD DAYS IN PARAGOULD.

"When I go to feed horses, they don't complain if I'm 30 minutes late," he said. "They're just tickled to death to see me walk through the barn door. Watching the babies eat and grow is one of my biggest joys. When I come back from the barn, it's like I'm a new person."

Brent's love for horses goes back to his childhood days in Paragould. His grandfather gave him two $100 horses for his 10th birthday, which he broke by himself. After six months of patient poking and prodding, he trained them to cross a creek near his home. Yet even though he enjoyed riding them, he dreamed of someday owning quality horses that he would be proud to show.

He began raising horses in 1990, soon after he was married. He said he "started from scratch and worked his way up," paying $400 and $425 respectfully for his first two horses. Recently, at a January sale, he bought a mare for several thousand dollars.

Today, Brent's cutting horses exhibit top bloodlines, some carrying the brand from the King Ranch in Texas. He currently stands at stud a son of Dry Doc, and has raised some excellent foals from him.

"I've have a good set of mares on the place right now that I never dreamed I would have the good fortune to own," Brent said. "It's exciting to think that I used to have junk, and now I'm getting calls from people out of state who are interested in buying my horses. It makes me feel good that they think I have something good enough for them to call and ask me about."

Even though Brent has not had any formal horse education, he has been through the school of hard knocks, earning his share of bruises and broken bones while breaking horses. When he first started, he would throw a rope around a horse's neck and let it drag him around the pasture.

< 1 4 4 >

"I used to go into it like a gunslinger," he said, laughing. "Now, I've learned that the calmer I stay, the better it is. Horses can be flighty. If you back them into a corner, they're going to go somewhere, maybe through a wall or over it."

Brent thinks his single-minded determination to raise quality horses has come from a solid work ethic handed down to him by his father and grandfather. He said that during his childhood when his father got through delivering mail every day, he would help him feed the cattle, tend to the hogs and work on the truck.

His grandfather, now 84, inspires him to work hard with his horses, but to use shortcuts whenever possible.

"He taught me that there's an easy way to do most everything," Brent said. "When I would try to fling a 150 pound bag of grain on the truck, he could get it into the back without actually having to lift it."

After Brent bought the land for his new home, he said his grandfather spent the entire winter bulldozing it, clearing out stumps and building roads leading up to his barn. Brent said he didn't ask him to do the work; it was just something he wanted to do for his grandson.

"I just hope I can do half of what he does when I get to be his age," Brent said. "Right now, he could probably work me into the ground."

Brent delights in his close-knit family ties, especially those he shares with his wife, Laura, his son, Tyner, born in 1999, and his daughter, Gena, born in 1996.

"Brent loves his horses, but he loves his family first," Laura said.

Gena said she enjoys traveling with her dad to the horse shows, and often helps out by cooling off the gelding in the walking ring after her father has finished riding.

> "I JUST HOPE I CAN DO HALF OF WHAT HE DOES WHEN I GET TO BE HIS AGE."

Brent said his daughter likes the horse because it's so gentle.

"That horse is so used to having to mind, he doesn't know there's a little girl on the top of him," he said. "Whenever she touches those reins, it's like she has power steering."

<145>

Brent said he likes the cutting horse business because it is so family-oriented. He said that like Gena, other children visit the shows and cool off the horses. He said that at a Batesville, Mississippi show, a lady was giving away homemade cookies in big plastic tubs and that the shows have a "county fair" atmosphere.

"I hope my daughter and son will enjoy horses all through their growing up years," he said. "When they get older this is something we can do together on weekends…and it may keep them out of trouble. So many things in this world today are bad. When I was growing up, I never saw the kids whose families were in the horse business uptown causing problems. They were always at the horse show with their parents."

Brent said he also likes attending horse shows because the people there treat him as an equal and that a natural bond exists because of their mutual interest in horses.

"The one thing that impresses me is that when I go to a horse show, I may see Alice Walton, whose father owned Wal-Mart, sitting on the back of a horse," he said. "This lady is worth billions of dollars and she's like the average Joe."

> A NATURAL BOND EXISTS BECAUSE OF THEIR MUTUAL INTEREST IN HORSES.

His new goal is to be a top breeder of Quarter horses, but he admitted, "it takes time to get there." In the meantime, he chooses to make money by attending horse sales.

Horse raising, Brent said, has taught him discipline and attention to detail. For example, he said he remembers the time a stable gate was accidentally left open. When he got home from work a gelding that had won $140,000 was standing in the hallway of the barn. At the time, his ranch didn't have any fences to keep in the horses.

"This horse could have wandered off," he said. "We were fortunate that he was so familiar with the barn that he didn't want to leave."

Brent acknowledged that he has learned patience and persistence through trial and error with the long horse-raising process. After one of his mares is bred, it takes a year for her to produce a foal. Then, he must wait another two years before he can ride it, and another one and a half years to show it.

<146>

BRENT MCCULLAR

"I consider myself a gung-ho, 'let's-get-it-done' type of person, and that's not always good," he said. "I've had to learn to slow down and not get in a big hurry, so that I can make sure the process is done the right way."

> "I'VE HAD TO LEARN TO SLOW DOWN AND NOT GET IN A BIG HURRY."

<147>

MOLLY MCELWEE

STUBBORN FIRE

If you ask Molly McElwee about her horse, Pal, she will tell you a wild and colorful tale of friendship with a horse that has brought her a fair amount of grief, but an even greater amount of joy.

"When I got sick, everyone asked me if I was angry at God," said Molly. "I couldn't, because I felt God has always been so kind to me, that God has always looked out for me and because my life has been so good. God gave me the opportunity to have a horse like Pal."

But no one had intended for Molly to ride Pal. In 1980 the 2-year-old, 16-hand 3-inch, double-registered Morgan and Palomino was a huge horse for tiny, 9-year-old Molly O'Kane. But now they are inseparable.

Molly's parents had purchased Pal for Molly's older brother, Hank, but he had grown tired of riding him. So Molly shared the horse with an

<149>

older sister who rode Pal in dressage. However, her sister got married and Molly had the horse all to herself – the only condition was that Molly could not alter Pal's dressage training. Of course, the dressage method was well beyond the capabilities of a 9-year-old.

THERE WAS BLOOD ALL OVER THE STABLE.

Molly spent her late adolescent and teenage years in her hometown of Golden, Colorado, disturbing the structured routine of the local riding team, the Westernaires, with her out-of-control horse. Because Pal was so large and Molly so small, she had a lot of difficulty controlling him. Moreover, because of his dressage training, she could not pull back on the horse or kick him to control him. Molly took a lot of criticism over her wild horse. Some thought that the horse's natural gifts and strengths were wasted on a teenage girl. But Molly tried to ignore the criticism and continued to lovingly work with her horse. Nevertheless, Pal had a mind of his own and Molly had a hard time convincing him to work with her, not against her.

However, one day, everything changed.

One morning, Molly went to the stables and found that an emotionally disturbed person had injured some of the horses. One of the horses was on the ground, cut in the neck, and there was blood all over the stable.

Molly quickly checked Pal and found blood all over his back leg. Molly was only 14 and didn't really understand what had happened. Since Molly's mother was a nurse, Molly decided to let her look at him. Molly walked the horse about a mile to their home. But with every step, Pal was bleeding his life away.

When she finally got to her house, her mother quickly assessed the severity of the situation and called the vet. The disturbed man had given Pal a 10-inch long gash, four inches deep, on the inside of his back leg. They anesthetized the horse and performed emergency surgery on the front lawn of their suburban home. One of his small arteries had been severed, but fortunately, no tendons had been cut.

Following surgery, they had to keep Pal in a special barn and Molly had to perform wound treatments that were very painful to him. Molly's mother, who is terrified of horses, had to try and hold the horse still while Molly tended the wound.

"As a kid I never realized that my parents had to sacrifice so much for me to keep my horse," Molly said.

Both of Molly's parents had to work two jobs to make ends meet – and on top of that, they paid for the upkeep and health of her horse. They even paid for very expensive surgery for Pal when it would have been easier and much cheaper to put him down.

After this ordeal, things greatly improved between Molly and Pal.

"That was a turning point in our relationship," she said.

While other kids were doing normal high school things, Molly and her friends in the Westernaires would take long rides into the nearby mountains. In addition, Molly used to ride some everyday and would usually spend at least five to eight hours at a time on horseback every Saturday.

"Once you spend that much time on a horse, it becomes your friend, your companion," she said.

"The sense of having something that large and that powerful respond to you – not because you could have any control over it, but because of a sense of duty, loyalty and friendship – is a gift that you get by putting in the effort," Molly said.

While Molly was in college, one of the things she did to make extra money was to teach children how to ride horses. One of her students had cerebral palsy and another was usually confined to a wheelchair. Both children loved the feeling of riding a powerful and beautiful animal and being free of the restrictions of their weakened bodies.

Beyond all of the activities and social events, Pal became Molly's best friend through high school and college.

"AS A KID I NEVER REALIZED THAT MY PARENTS HAD TO SACRIFICE SO MUCH FOR ME TO KEEP MY HORSE."

"If I had a problem or I broke up with my boyfriend, I would talk about it to Pal," she said.

Nevertheless, the horse was not kind to Molly's boyfriends.

"He chased away about five of them," she said. "He would knock them down with his head and then walk between them and me."

One ex-boyfriend told her," You're never going to get married until that horse dies." However, that turned out not to be true.

One day, Molly organized a horse ride for single adults in her

<151>

church and a young man named David McElwee decided to join them.

"I guess when Dave saw me on Pal he was impressed because Pal is such a dynamic horse. I was so comfortable with Pal that I was sitting sideways on him and Dave thought that I must be amazing to ride a horse like that. He didn't know that I fell out of the saddle uncountable times," she said.

David proposed, and the happy couple made plans to marry. About six months before their wedding, Dave asked Molly if she wanted to keep Pal. Molly's response was direct.

"I'd probably part with you before I'd part with my horse," she said. "If you love me, you'll love my horse because he's so much a part of my identity."

Within a few weeks, Dave bought a horse of his own so that they could ride together. He also traded in his new Ford Explorer for a pickup truck to pull the horse trailer.

But shortly after their wedding, Dave and Molly McElwee faced a new challenge. Molly was diagnosed with Elhers-Danlos syndrome (EDS), Type III (hypermobility type).

> **"IF YOU LOVE ME, YOU'LL LOVE MY HORSE BECAUSE HE'S SO MUCH A PART OF MY IDENTITY."**

EDS is a group of hereditary disorders that primarily affects the skin and joints, but often affects other organs as well. Hypermobile joints, overly elastic skin and fragile body tissues characterize it. Occurring in both children and adults, experts estimate that somewhere between one in 5,000 to one in 10,000 people suffer from EDS, but the disease is often undiagnosed or misdiagnosed after symptoms occur.

People with EDS have a defect in the connective tissue that provides support to many parts of the body such as the skin, muscles, tendons and ligaments. In Molly's case, her ligaments don't work properly. As a result, she has had trouble with frequent damage and dislocation of her joints. She suffered from problems with dislocations throughout her days of horseback riding, but assumed that she was just clumsy. She also had chronic and sometimes debilitating pain in her joints.

"Growing up, there was a sense that something was wrong," she said. She instinctively became more cautious as she grew older.

<152>

Unfortunately, she was originally prescribed the wrong treatment for her symptoms and it accelerated the progress of the disease. And the disease progressed to the point that she was unable to continue her nursing career. She also almost lost Pal.

Riding puts an enormous strain on Molly's joints. Sitting on a wide horse like Pal threatens to pull her hips out of their sockets.

"When I lost my career and lost being a nurse, the doctors told Dave that he had to get me off horses," she said. "But Dave knew that it was so much a part of my identity that I would not stop riding. Dave promised me that he would never make me give up my horses."

> "DAVE PROMISED ME THAT HE WOULD NEVER MAKE ME GIVE UP MY HORSES."

And Molly's doctors have changed their minds. Although they would never recommend riding to anyone in her condition, they have to admit that her spine is very healthy for someone with EDS, and they attribute that to all the years of horseback riding.

"The new approach to my treatment is to maximize what I can do to keep myself out of the wheelchair by being active," she said.

While Molly currently has to use two Canadian crutches to walk, she continues to ride Pal occasionally. She can only ride for about thirty minutes at a time. "But riding Pal is easier than walking," she said.

"When you've ridden a horse for 20 years, you can sense what they are going to do and what they are not going to do," she said. "Pal looks really good for his age. Though he's got a sway back and he's really cranky, I still see him as the horse he was.

"It's pure joy to ride Pal now. It transcends him being an old cripple and me being a young cripple…you forget all that and it's like being back in the old days. It's very freeing for someone who is disabled. When I ride Pal, I am equal to everyone else because I'm a good rider. Nobody knows anything different. They don't see the canes. They don't have to treat me special if I'm on a horse.

"I've had a lot of people over the years tell me that I've ruined him. For a while I felt kind of embarrassed, but now I feel like a horse could not have had a better life. The horse wants to be in a relationship where he is loved. I don't think a horse could have been loved more."

<153>

MIKE & MARRITA MCMILLIAN

FOR THE LOVE
OF HORSES

Mike and Marrita McMillian live for and with horses. He trains them; she sculpts them.

Horses were their matchmakers. And today they are both their vocations and their avocations.

But the McMillian's are by no means species-exclusive with their time. They enjoy a large circle of friends and acquaintances met through their activities with horses.

"So many good people work and participate in the horse industry," Mike said. "They're honest, hard-working, reliable people you enjoy knowing. And they teach those traits to their kids."

Husband and wife were first introduced to horses early in life.

"My mother says I learned to say 'horse' before I learned to say

<155>

'Mama',," Marrita said.

The first horse Marrita referred to was an old draft animal on her grandfather's farm. She would ride the horse on weekends with her grandparents. Luck introduced her to another horse when her mother won a pony. The pony was boarded at a nearby stable and cemented Marrita's affection for horses.

"BASICALLY, I LOVE ALL ANIMALS...D DOGS, CATS, LAMBS."

"Basically, I love all animals...dogs, cats, lambs," she said. "But I appreciate that horses are big and beautiful and I like being around them."

Marrita said that when she out grew the pony, her mother bought her a gray gelding.

"He was so old and broken down, but I tried to show him anyway," she said. "I was young. I didn't know better."

She said her next horse was Shyloah Lou. Together they entered and began to gain recognition at American Quarter Horse Association open shows. During her high school years, she began to train horses for other people. She became a registered trainer and worked with horses all through her college years. She couldn't afford a show-level horse of her own, but often took other people's horses to shows and rode for them.

Marritta met her husband Mike at one of these shows. And they kept meeting at horse shows.

"I guess you could say we courted at the horse shows," Mike said.

Mike became acquainted with animals early. His father trained hunting dogs. When Mike was 6, his dad began training horses. This led Mike into horse training, which he did through his high school and college years. This, of course, is what got him to those horse shows where he met his wife.

"We had so much in common," Marrita said, "and so much to talk about."

The talk led to marriage and a horse training business. They own and operate McMillian Quarter Horses, Inc. in Gainesville, Texas. They also reared a daughter who is, can you guess, a horse trainer.

"We concentrate on halter horses and show at the local, state, and national levels," Mike said.

The couple have educational backgrounds geared to the horse

<156>

business. Mike earned a degree in animal science from Oklahoma State in Stillwater, Oklahoma. Marrita earned a similar degree from Missouri Western University in St. Joseph.

"We are basically a training operation," Mike said. "We do act as agent for some of our clients, but training is our main mission."

And training, he said, is what they do best. Mike has been training and showing horses for about 40 years.

"We feel fortunate to have a job that is also our hobby," Mike said. "Training horses is what we like to do. And if we work hard at it, we make money. You can't beat making money doing something you love to do anyway."

That being the case it's no surprise to learn the McMillians enjoy "working" vacations. Mike is a sought-after judge at horse shows around the world, something he's been doing for 18 years.

"We like to go snow skiing, too, but we don't get to very often," Mike said. "The horses and training take up most of our time."

He said his favorite part of the business is "Watching the young people and the amateurs do well in the show ring. About 99 percent of our clients are youth and/or amateurs. We work with some kids who are only 8 or 9 years old. Halter horses are the easiest for beginners. It gets them started."

"THE HORSES AND TRAINING TAKE UP MOST OF OUR TIME."

The couple is also active in the American Quarter Horse Youth Foundation and the Professional Horseman's Association. They are life members of both organizations.

Mike said that in working with kids he has seen some grow to love horses just as he does. For them, he has some advice.

"Stay in school. Finish college, then take an internship with a teacher or trainer. See if you like it and are good enough to make a living at it. Besides, being an intern with someone already in the business is a great way to launch your own career."

The McMillans have helped launch a number of careers in the horse industry. There are usually two or three interns working at the their ranch. A recent intern spent three years with them before leaving to start his own business.

<157>

For an avocation, Mike collects antique horse equipment and memorabilia. Traveling to judge horse shows allows him to find rare and/or unique items from the early days of horse shows, horse racing and rodeos. His collection is on display at the McMillian ranch.

Marrita's avocation has become a second vocation. She sculpts horses. Her bronze work can be found in galleries and museums across the country, and in private collections throughout the world.

She has always had an interest in art. She took art classes in high school, but was discouraged by a teacher who was more interested in "modern" art than realism. She didn't take art in college, but modeled for painting classes. There she picked up tips on technique and style. When the art classes began to use nude models, Marrita said she stopped modeling and art took a back seat to horses.

She said that in 1992 she and a friend were visiting galleries in Santa Fe, New Mexico when she realized the work they were admiring was great, but didn't reflect the confirmation of modern-day Quarter horses.

"I wanted art that represented horses today," she said. "I didn't want to recreate Remington (western artist Frederick Remington). The confirmation of today's horse is more elegant, refined and beautiful. Among other things, they are sleeker and have thinner necks. I can look at a piece of art, either sculpture or painting, and tell you what century or era the work is from just by looking at the rendering of the horse."

"THE CONFIRMATION OF TODAY'S HORSE IS MORE ELEGANT, REFINED AND BEAUTIFUL."

The Santa Fe experience, she said, prompted her to go back to her art.

She said, "There wasn't anybody representing today's horses, cowboys, and cowgirls. I knew I could."

And represent them she can. Her work is on display at The American Quarter Horse Association Heritage Center and Museum in Amarillo, Texas. And the American Paint Horse Association has commissioned her to produce a piece for the front of their headquarters in Fort Worth, Texas.

Motion picture actor Arnold Schwarzeneger and a former Miss America have also purchased her work.

MIKE & MARRITA MCMILLIAN

She has sculpted the 2000 Olympic halter-horse winners and is producing porcelain sculptures of the most influential American Quarter Horse Champions for the Breyer Animal Creations collection. The first release was the infamous racing pair, Kip Diderickson and Refrigerator.

Marrita displays her work at a number of prominent horse shows, such as the Quarter Horse Congress and the American Quarter Horse World Show. Her studio is located at the McMillian ranch.

Mike and Marrita live and work for the love of horses. Any horse-lovers living or traveling in the Gainesville, Texas area are invited to drop by to see the horses, the antiques and the art on display at McMillian Quarter Horses, Inc.

> MARRITA DISPLAYS HER WORK AT A NUMBER OF PROMINENT HORSE SHOWS.

<159>

DAN & CAROL MCWHIRTER

A SIMPLE
TWIST OF FATE

Dan McWhirter used to think he would end up being a corn and soybean farmer, tending land in his native Nebraska as his ancestors had always done with, possibly, one exception. He and his wife, Carol, would, perhaps, operate a modest horse business.

However, fate and a conscientious work ethic enabled the Doniphan native and Carol to become the leading quarter horse breeders of the most performance class winners in the country today.

The lives of the couple changed when their good friend, Pam Snow, visited them in the '80s. For a tax shelter Pam's brother, Dr. John Hilton of San Diego, California, wanted to invest $50,000 in a quality stallion.

Pam pestered the McWhirters to look for such a horse, to buy it

<161>

and to stand it as a stud at their farm. Until then Dan and Carol had not been in the stallion business, but at Pam's insistence they seriously began their quest for just the right horse.

Initially they felt as if their mission might end up like the search for the proverbial "needle in a haystack," but fate smiled on them.

THEY HAD SEEN A CHAMP-IONSHIP QUALITY STALLION NAMED THE BIG INVESTMENT.

Even before Pam had asked for their help, the McWhirters had attended a quarter horse show in Belleville, Kansas, where they had seen a championship quality stallion named The Big Investment.

Their eyes had popped when they saw the handsome, charismatic horse of 16 hands, along with three of his offspring that looked exactly the same.

"The stallion 'cookie-cut' his colts," Carol said. "That's the sign of pre-potency, and you don't find it too often. People often breed a world champion stallion to some wonderful mares, and when the colts come, they look like Heinz 57s. They're not stamped with uniformity or quality."

Carol knew in her heart that this special stallion was the one for the Hiltons, but there was a problem. Owner Don Fritzler of Hanston, Kansas, wanted $150,000 for the prize stallion.

Determined to buy The Big Investment, the McWhirters located another partner, "Dutch" Gay, an attorney from O'Neill, Nebraska. With Dr. Hilton, Gay and Pam Snow, the McWhirters formed a syndicate.

Meanwhile, the horse's owner came down on his price.

In his two short years standing at the McWhirters farm, The Big Investment lived up to his potential. By 1997 his foals had earned a substantial $320,313 in futurity and AQHA Incentive. And at the 1990 All-American Quarter Horse Congress, four of the Top 10 finishers in the 3-Year-Old Snaffle Bit Futurity were sired by The Big Investment.

In 1986, Dan and Carol thought the best was yet to come for their 6-year-old stallion. But on an August night that year when Dan was making his rounds, he noticed that The Big Investment was standing with his head facing the corner of his stall. The drastic change in the barometric pressure brought about by a huge low-pressure center

<162>

moving through Nebraska had triggered a severe case of intestinal colic.

Dan immediately called the vet, who monitored the horse for several hours before recommending that he be taken to Kansas State University, a five-hour drive. Within ten minutes of their arrival at the university, the magnificent stallion collapsed and died.

After this horrible tragedy the McWhirters were so devastated emotionally and financially that they almost quit the horse business.

However, for Dan and Carol what was perceived as an awful calamity turned into a life-changing experience.

"There was a reason for the horse dying, but we didn't understand it at the time," Carol said. "We gathered ourselves together and diligently pursued buying his father, The Invester, so we could give him a home for the rest of his life."

In his earlier years The Invester was a superior halter horse, garnering a total of 29 Grand Championships and 16 Reserve Championships. He was the third all-time leading sire of performance Register of Merit qualifiers, finishing behind his half-brother Zippo Pine-Bar and Two Eyed Jack.

The Invester had sired three world champions – El Cicatriz, the 1974 Youth World Champion yearling gelding; We Are Magic, the 1980 World Champion weanling mare; and Impulsions, the 1989 2-year-old Western Pleasure Champion.

Twenty years old in 1989, The Invester appeared to be at the end of his stud career when the unthinkable happened. His partial owner and syndicate manager, Jack Benson of Brenham, Texas, was traveling to a horse show in Katy, Texas. He stepped out of his pickup on the side of the highway and was hit by a truck and killed.

A few weeks after Benson's death the McWhirters contacted his widow and told her about their ownership of The Big Investment, the son of The Invester, and the tragedy that had befallen them. They told her they would be interested in buying The Invester if he was ever for sale. She promised to call them if she decided to sell.

"WE GATHERED OURSELVES TOGETHER AND DILI-GENTLY PURSUED BUYING HIS FATHER, THE INVESTER."

"We had complete faith that, because we had called early and

<163>

were on the list, we would be notified when the horse came up for sale," Carol said. "This was not the case."

According to Carol, this is where fate came in. One September day in1989, Carol went to famous breeder Howard Pitzer's annual production sale, which was at his ranch just 80 miles north of the McWhirter farm. There she ran into Chuck Wilson, a horse breeder from Texas who had raised Impulsions, at the time the most recent world champion offspring of The Invester.

She recalls Chuck asking, "Carol, did you hear that The Invester is up for sale now?"

"My jaw dropped," Carol said. "This just had to be fate. At a horse sale in Nebraska, I just happened to run into a Texan who knew about the horse coming on the market."

Excited, Carol raced home to tell Dan the good news. The next morning, she called Mrs. Benson to inquire about the price, but because of her grief the widow was unable to discuss such things. She, instead, had Dale Livingston, a horseman friend of the family, call Carol back. He arranged the sale.

"CAROL, DID YOU HEAR THAT THE INVESTER IS UP FOR SALE NOW?"

After getting a partner, Wayne Atchley of Elkhorn, Nebraska, to put up half of the money, the McWhirters immediately sent the deposit for the horse. They then made plans to pick the animal up. They gassed up their truck, hitched their horse trailer to it and made sure all was ready for their trip to the Benson's Stallions Unlimited ranch at Brenham.

But the night before their planned departure the following morning, Mrs. Benson called to say that she had changed her mind and was selling to someone else.

Carol said that after three months of intense legal maneuvering they were finally able to complete their purchase of The Invester. But by the time he could be shipped from Texas to Nebraska, she said, he was weakened from malnutrition and neglect.

"We promptly called an equine dentist in to work on his teeth," Carol said. "The horse was 21 years old when we got him and, to our relief, he started recovering and gaining his weight back. He wasn't perfect when the breeding season came around, but he was in much bet-

<164>

ter condition than when we got him. The truth is that we saved the horse's life."

Carol firmly believes that it was their destiny to acquire the aged horse and nurse him back to health.

"People told us not to buy The Invester because he was a has-been," she said. "But there was never a doubt in our minds about going forward. That horse needed us, and we needed him."

In the twilight years of his life, the old stallion has proved everyone wrong by producing many of his best offspring, including the five Congress Champions Iota Invest, Assets, Vested Pine, Invester's Fancy Doll, and Investor's Style. His last two foals hit the ground in 1999, and he is officially retired. His legacy truly lives on in his colts, and his notoriety has literally made the McWhirters famous.

> "IT'S HARD TO BELIEVE THAT ONE HORSE COULD MAKE THAT KIND OF DIFFER-ENCE."

"It's hard to believe that one horse could make that kind of difference," Carol enthused. "We have travelers stopping by all the time to see the horse. It's like a celebrity living around here."

Dan and Carol laugh about how The Invester, born in 1969, is so set in his ways.

"He rules the roost," Dan said. "Whatever he wants, he gets."

Special treatment involves turning him out every day at the same time in an outdoor pen.

Dan laughed and said, "If people want to see him outside later in the day, he may choose not to come out of his stall because he's been out already."

"He's like an old grandfather," Carol said. "He's an aristocrat that knows he's a special horse. He has dignity, charisma and an air about him. A couple of months ago I nicknamed him the Chairman of the Board."

Carol said that at 10 o'clock every night The Invester has to have his "oatmeal snack," a chore that often falls to the McWhirters teenage son, Daniel, when the couple are away.

The McWhirters have been married since 1979, and about her husband Carol said, "He's like the Rock of Gibraltar. Dan's the man who makes this all happen. Whether he feels good or not, he's out there doing the job every day."

<165>

FRANK MERRILL

MICHIGAN COWBOY

Frank Merrill is a horseman by choice – not birth.

"I was sort of the black sheep of the family…I was the only cowboy," recalled the Michigan native, who now speaks with something of an Oklahoma drawl. "All I can tell you is my mother said the first word out of my mouth as a baby was 'horse.' I was born and raised in Michigan, but I wanted to grow up and move out West and be a cowboy. It's all I ever talked about. I never wavered from my goal."

Merrill owns and operates Windward Stud, a commercial breed farm in Purcell, Oklahoma. The horseman's mother actually named the ranch.

"The wind was blowing hard when I was showing her the property," he said. "We were talking about a name for it, and she said, 'I'll

<167>

tell you one damn thing, it ought to have the wind in it. Why don't you call it Windward?' "

Windward Stud breeds 350 to 500 mares a year – and raises, trains, breeds, buys and sells its own horses. Merrill estimates that since 1972 it has stood about 76 stallions and bred more than 16,000 mares. It presently stands seven cutting horse stallions:

MERRILL SAID REPUTATION IS THE RANCH'S MOST PRIZED POSSESSION.

• Bobby Bo Badger (owned by Merrill)
• Doc Olena Twist (owned by Merrill and Mark Lavender)
• Little Trona (owned by Benjie Neely)
• Mr. Skyline Peppy (owned by James Hooper)
• Quanah Olena (owned by Merrill and Warren Miller)
• Starlight's Joy (owned by Merrill and Ken Smith Jr.)
• Young Gun (owned by Terry and Sharon Riddle)

"We are involved with roping, reining and racing as well. But our main thrust is cutting horses."

Merrill said reputation is the ranch's most prized possession. And it certainly doesn't hurt to have two horses inducted into the American Quarter Horse Association Hall of Fame in the year 2000.

Merrill has owned Miss Jim 45 since his early days.

"She's considered to be one of the greatest halter mares that ever lived," he said.

And Royal Santana earned reviews as one of the all-time cutting greats.

Merrill's entire family is involved in showing – and in winning big. Merrill and his wife Robin compete in National Cutting Horse Association shows, while their children – McKenzie, Megan and Tyler compete in AQHA shows across the country.

"Each one of us in this family has earned at least one world championship in AQHA competition," he said, "which is one of our greatest achievements as a family. All my kids and my wife and I have won numerous titles in NCHA competitions."

Merrill also has won votes outside the competition ring. He is a Cowboy Hall of Fame board member, AQHA director, Stud Book

<168>

FRANK MERRILL

Registration Committee member, Oklahoma Quarter Horse Association past president and current director, member of the St. John's Northwestern Military Academy board of trustees in Delafield, Wisconsin and a trustee for the Dogwood Foundation, a charitable foundation based in Florida.

But it almost didn't play out this well for the Michigan cowboy. It wasn't that Merrill had a particularly hard ride to the top of his industry. He just had a tough time hanging on during the raucous '80s.

"I've been riding horses since I was 5 years old," Merrill said. "I've been serious about it since I was 16."

He apprenticed with such noted horsemen as George Tyler, Mattlock Rose and Jerry Wells, until he decided he was ready to go solo. He bought his ranch in 1971. He was 23.

"The original property consisted of 100 acres," he said. "I owned a stallion named Boston Mac at the time, a racehorse/halter horse that we stood primarily to halter horse mares. I started laying the buildings out and building the fence during the course of '71 and '72. We had our first formal breeding season in '73. And I've been building on it ever since."

Merrill said the best way to generate business is to associate with the very best horses possible.

"So quality has always been the main thrust here as far as the type of livestock we have and raise," he said.

The ranch stood both racehorses and cutting horses.

"As racing became more popular and lucrative," he said, "we became more and more involved."

THE BEST WAY TO GENERATE BUSINESS IS TO ASSOCIATE WITH THE VERY BEST HORSES POSSIBLE.

Windward Stud reached its prime and near demise, he said, in the '80s when it stretched across almost 500 acres and stood 15 racehorse stallions. Each year mares were bred by the thousands.

Until 1986.

The Tax Reform of 1986 and the oil bust put the brakes on the racing industry.

Hard.

"Purcell, Oklahoma was like the Lexington of the quarter horse industry for many, many years," he said. "Most of the stud farms were right here. That was probably the biggest part of our economy in this county."

The combination of the tax reform, oil bust and racing skid brought the county to its knees.

"When the dust settled, Merrill said, Windward Stud was the only farm left standing "and we were barely hanging on. We were very close to shutting our doors."

What spared Windward?

"Perseverance," Merrill said, adding, "We were very fortunate to have some contacts that could help us get by until we could repay the banks and restructure our business."

Like the rest of the country, Purcell slowly rebounded. And so did Windward, by switching saddles to performance horses.

"There's been a definite renaissance in the county and community that really surrounds the performance horse," Merrill said, noting that once empty ranches are now full of reiners, cutters and the like. "It's like a drought occurred, then the rains came, cleansed the earth and now the grass is growing again."

> "IT'S LIKE A DROUGHT OCCURRED, THEN THE RAINS CAME, CLEANSED THE EARTH AND NOW THE GRASS IS GROWING AGAIN."

But growing at a much more controlled pace. Windward Stud, he said, is back down to a more manageable 140 acres, and it just stands pure stallions. And Merrill and his crew are much wiser for the experience, having learned not to swim too far away from shore.

"Today we're not operating such a large enterprise," he said. "We try to concern ourselves with more quality than quantity. We have always, and always will, treat our customers like they're part of our family. We treat their horses as good as our own. We always give them an honest appraisal of their situation and try to help them make good economic decisions with their livestock."

Looking back, Merrill said if he could have foreseen 1986, he would have played it a lot smarter.

<170>

FRANK MERRILL

"Even though I knew it was coming," he said, "I didn't think it would affect us because our business was so good. Little did I know. But I got smart in a hurry."

His advice to others is the same that one of his mentors offered early on.

"I think the best advice," he said, "is what George Tyler told me long ago: 'Never ever compromise your ideals and quality. And always buy the very best you can afford.' "

> "NEVER EVER COMPRO-MISE YOUR IDEALS AND QUALITY."

<171>

GARY & COLLEEN MILLER

FOCUSED VISION

Colleen Miller vividly recalls her first memory of horses. It was created as she lay face down in the mud, just after a Morgan she had been riding for a week had thrown her off.

"I was 8 years old," she said. "My uncle had two riding horses, a Morgan and a Quarter Horse. The Morgan broke my back. She ran off when my cousin was riding on a bike next to her and spooked her. I couldn't even walk for two years. That was my first memory...in 1948."

But she mounted a horse again as soon as she could and hasn't strayed from the animals since. Although her mother didn't have a fondness for horses – in fact, she couldn't stand them – it was Colleen's paternal grandmother, Jesse Kenyon, from whom she inherited her

<173>

love for the animals. She and her family visited the farm each summer and she soon learned that people either like horses or they don't.

Colleen said she learned how to ride and care for horses from her grandmother and her uncle. There were no instructors nearby. In fact, she did not receive formal instruction until her first year in college when a friend, Joanne, took a week to teach her some riding techniques.

> "YOU COULDN'T TAKE A COURSE ON HORSES, BECAUSE THEY DID NOT OFFER ONE."

Focused on her vision of raising horses, Colleen was one of only three women to study animal husbandry at Michigan State University at the time she was in college.

"It was a study of cattle, sheep and pigs," she said. You couldn't take a course on horses, because they did not offer one."

She had three Quarter horses and rode for other people to make extra money on the side. Her weekends were spent traveling to shows in Indiana, Ohio and other states competing in every event from jumping to conformation.

She had been raising and showing horses 10 years before she met her husband, Gary. Although she had known the women in his family for years – they all had their hair done at her mother's salon – she had never met Gary. He was a city boy. But she sold both he and a friend a 2-year-old Poco Pine gelding shortly after they were discharged from the Marine Corps.

"They didn't know a thing about horses," she said. "The geldings they purchased, Wamps Palo Pine and Pines 007, weren't even broke, but these guys were so fit after coming out of the Marines that they just jumped on them and rode them.

"Gary's horse was a Palomino. And a lot of people, if they've never had a horse, love Palominos. The horses ended up with about 400 points.

"Maybe that's why I liked the horses," she said when remembering her childhood days helping her mother at the beauty shop. "I heard every story in town there, but horses don't spread rumors, and they appreciate it when they're treated well."

At the time Colleen met Gary, she said she had a lot of brood

<174>

mares. After they became engaged, they purchased a farm with a 150-year-old house and barn about a month before the wedding.

"I was afraid I was going to end up in an apartment in the city," she said, laughing.

Skylane Farm, which they purchased, is located in Dewitt, Michigan, just 10 miles north of the farm where Colleen grew up. It was originally named for its geographical location directly at the end of Lansing's Capitol City Airport runway.

The 120-acre farm has raised and sold World Champions, Reserve World Champions (Ojibway, Silky Socks, Purf Bar Midge 108 and Secure For Years) Honor Roll Champions (too many to mention), AQHA Champions, Congress Champions, PHBA Champions and dozens of State Champions.

Colleen's and Gary's son, Bob, has followed in his parents' footsteps. He loves horses and began showing at an early age. He was also very active in the Youth World competitions, which they all continue to support. Today, he shows amateur and open and has done very well.

"I never wanted him to be a professional," Colleen said of their son. "I've seen too many professional horsemen that have just gone broke, only about three percent of them make it. I never would let him train with a pro when he was showing pleasure because I thought if he couldn't learn it here and do it himself, then he won't remember it all. Bob finally watched all of his friends that rode with pros stop showing after completing their youth career. But he just loves his horses. His present show horse, Secure For Years, was fit and trained by Bob. For four years Bob checked on him at 11 p.m., to make sure he was OK. The 'do it yourself' tactic really paid off. Some of their accomplishments include 1998 High point stallion in the Nation, 1998 Congress Champion 1998 Reserve World Champion, Honor Roll High Point."

> "I WAS AFRAID I WAS GOING TO END UP IN AN APARTMENT IN THE CITY."

In 2000, Colleen traveled to Fort Worth, Texas to support kids from Michigan in the Youth World Championships. Although she used to train young riders and their horses, she now goes to the com-

<175>

petitions to provide support.

The future holds more of the same for Skylane Farm. They have 15 head and were expecting four babies in spring of 2001.

That's plenty, Colleen said, because she can handle that many and still have time for gardening and other hobbies, while Gary can step away from his day job and the barn work to catch a round of golf.

"We've never wanted to be real big to where we didn't have time for the family," she said. "We try to keep it on a smaller scale, and yet for over 30 years we have been at the top of our classes at the largest shows in a variety of events."

> "WE'VE NEVER WANTED TO BE REAL BIG TO WHERE WE DIDN'T HAVE TIME FOR THE FAMILY."

Colleen said she also takes off every year to ride with a group of women called Las Caballeras through the trails of California.

"I couldn't do that if we had 50 to 80 head," Colleen said. "You just quit enjoying it when it gets overwhelming.

"There's so many people (at the shows) that don't even have horses anymore, but they just can't get away from it. They have made so many friends nationally and internationally. The common interest keeps everyone together.

"In our last 30 plus years at Skylane Farm we have never regretted doing 98 percent of the horse business the 'do-it-yourself' way. Our customers have come to realize that our horses are the 'real' deal and not the product of professionals with politics."

< 1 7 6 >

<177>

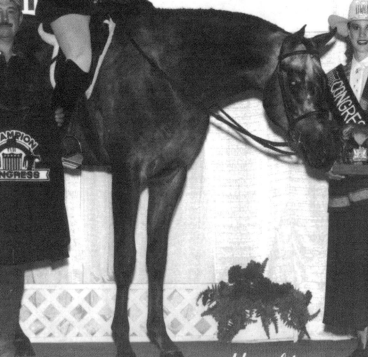

1996

ALL AMERICAN
QUARTER HORSE
CONGRESS

Harold
Campton

RAY & LINDA MONACO

LIVING IN
PROSPERITY

Quarter Horse breeders Ray and Linda Monaco can truly say they're living in Prosperity – the "blink and you miss it town" of Prosperity, Pennsylvania, that is.

"The name of the town really fits us," Linda said. "Our luck has been very good here. We are very fortunate that our babies have met all of our expectations."

Linda loves the quiet, scenic countryside that she calls home. She feels that she's in "God's country" every time she takes her early morning walk over the rolling green hills. Often she sees wildlife, including turkeys with their babies in tow, deer and rabbits, because she is out "in the middle of nowhere."

Viewing gorgeous scenery is nothing new for Linda. She grew up

<179>

"between two waters" in historic Easton, Maryland, near the Chesapeake Bay. Her twin sister, Sandra, still lives there.

Linda said she got started with horses when she was 5 years old. Her father, a county extension agent, took Sandra and her with him on his farm visits. The farmers who owned horses would saddle up their old plow horses and let the girls ride them up and down their fence rows.

"IF WE WANTED SOMETHING, WE HAD TO WORK TO BUY IT."

When she and her sister turned 12, they worked and saved up $230 to buy a horse, saddle and bridle. After their initial investment, they continued to work after school and during summers to keep the horse. Linda said that both her father, a former Navy beach master stationed at Normandy during World War II, and mother, were very strict with them.

"If we wanted something, we had to work to buy it," she said. "I appreciate that about my parents, although I didn't back then."

Linda said she and her sister enjoyed riding with friends in a trail-riding club that sponsored "Old Time Fun Days". The duo soon got interested in "over the fence" fox hunts across the Maryland countryside.

"We were kamikaze pilots on horses," she said, laughing. "While riding through the woods, we would grab a branch, let it go, and the people behind us didn't stand a chance!"

As an active teenager Linda also enjoyed snow and water skiing and ice-skating. She compared her daredevil youth to "something out of a movie" because she said she always "lived on the edge." In fact, she said she saved her twin sister's life once during a heart-stopping horseback ride.

"My sister was riding a green, 3-year-old Appaloosa that didn't know what the weight of a rider felt like yet," she said. "The horse bolted and headed toward two-lane traffic on the highway. I came flying up, grabbed the bridle, and saved her, just like a scene out of a movie."

Linda gradually became more interested in Quarter horse shows during the '70s, and competed in Western pleasure events. She took lessons from Robert Newcomb of Preston, Maryland, a man she described as "an old and wise trainer" who taught her more about life

<180>

than riding.

"He had an insight that I could literally feel when I was around him," she said. "From him, I learned to set up my goals, and then aim for them. He was the building block to my desire to make working with horses a life rather than a maybe."

During the '80s Linda attended a community college, majoring in business. In 1987 she married Ray, a project superintendent for P. J. Dick, Inc., of Pittsburgh, Pennsylvania, who at the time was working on the coliseum at Wake Forest University in North Carolina.

Because of Ray's project-oriented job the couple moved often, but finally ended up residing at Hunters Ridge Farm in Prosperity.

Linda's favorite horse in the '80s was a 16.1 hand, dark chestnut all-around gelding, that was an only son of Storyman. So, of course, she nicknamed him Story.

"We spent a lifetime in just five years," she said. "He was like a buddy to me, because he followed me around like a big Great Dane and loved on me constantly. Maybe I spoiled him with too many sugar cubes."

Linda said she was forced to have a "diversified resume" because of their frequent moves. She has been a dental assistant, an interior decorator, an executive secretary, an accounting assistant, a title abstracter and an equine appraiser. All of this experience, combined with the solid work ethic handed down by her parents, has helped her with her bustling Quarter horse business.

> "MAYBE I SPOILED HIM WITH TOO MANY SUGAR CUBES."

On a normal day, Linda said she receives around 65 telephone calls from prospective customers, mare owners and friends, sometimes as late as midnight.

"I burn up three cordless phones a day, because I always have them hanging on my ear," she said.

Linda said she is very selective when placing her "Blue babies" with people because she wants to make sure the potential owners can do the proper promotion. So far her system has worked out well.

"I enjoy meeting people, so that's probably why I've been successful," she said. "If I was at a party 20 years ago, I would have been the most inconspicuous person in the room. It's funny how life has

<181>

changed me. Everyone has a story to tell, and I love to listen. Now life for me is filled with fun, new challenges, excitement and never-ending surprises."

She said talking to people on the phone and making sales is only part of her typical day. She has to get up at 5 a.m. to clean stalls, feed the mares along with their babies and check their condition, especially during the breeding season. Then she goes back to the office to take care of the book work, computer work and general upkeep that goes with maintaining a business.

Linda said that ever since she was a teenager, she had always admired big, exotic, slow-legged horses. So in 1994, Ray and Linda fulfilled their dream by purchasing Skys Blue Boy, a 17 hand charcoal gray stallion. He has won numerous championships and NSBA Futurities, such as the 1996 Congress/Millers Hunter Under Saddle and Superior award in Hunter Under Saddle, the 1997 Congress/Junior Hunter Under Saddle and the 1997 Open High Point/Hunter Under Saddle Stallion.

> "EVERYONE HAS A STORY TO TELL, AND I LOVE TO LISTEN."

In January of Blue's 3-year-old year, after much discussion and deliberation, the Monacos made the choice to send their horse to Patti and Jerry Robertson to promote him as a stallion and a show horse.

"We looked long and hard for the right trainer," Linda said. "We had admired the talents of Patti and Jerry for years from afar. We wanted the kind of training program for our horse that would produce success without sacrificing him. Patti has a presence that commands respect without her knowing it. I knew she would be the one to commit for the long haul."

Currently, Blue is standing at stud at Robertson Quarter Horses in Micanopy, Florida, near Ocala.

Linda said she feels that sensitivity in a person is nothing more than an awareness of what is going on, and she uses this quality all the time in her horse breeding.

"I have to use my eyes and observe each mare on a daily basis," she said. "I look for subtle changes in behavior. At foaling time, this could be the difference between life and death. Fortunately, we also

<182>

have a surveillance monitor in each stall, so we can watch them from our master bedroom, sometimes all night long, in anticipation of the new Blue arrivals." She and her husband do the birthing and only call the vet in when the mare has a problem delivery. For Monaco, the foals have taught her to be more patient and understanding.

Linda, born in 1955, believes that she is blessed to do what she loves every day.

"I'm a lucky person," she said. "I eat, sleep, and breathe horses, but it's what I love."

Skys Blue Boy winning the Miller Hunter Under Saddle 1996 fulfilled a lifelong dream for the Monacos – and the second big win the following year was like living a fairy tale.

"We are still living that dream, looking for the next Blue," Linda said.

> "I HAVE TO USE MY EYES AND OBSERVE EACH MARE ON A DAILY BASIS."

<183>

JEFF KIRKBRIDE Photography

JOHN NARMONT

THE TRUTH ABOUT HORSES

John Narmont said he was 6 or 7 years old when he got on a horse and the first thing he learned was that he didn't want to get off.

John's father maintained that his son's love for horses developed because he didn't have one of his own. John's father was a city-bound businessman active in farm equipment, real estate and banking. John's only chance to ride came while visiting an aunt who owned a farm an hour away from the family home in Auburn, Illinois.

"My aunt had two ponies," John recalled. "So whenever we would visit, I would literally ride one of them from the time we got there to the time we left."

The fascination continued as John, while in grade school, discovered a neighbor who kept a horse in a vacant lot. John would take

<185>

every opportunity to visit his neighbor and ride the horse.

It wasn't until much later, however, that John would indulge his early interest in horses. Finishing college and entering a law career took precedence. After graduating, he established a thriving law practice in his hometown of Auburn and nearby Springfield. Today the law practice encompasses a substantial part of the state of Illinois. He also participates in real estate and other business ventures with his family.

> "I'VE ALWAYS HAD A LOVE OF PALOMINO HORSES, SO I STARTED OUT IN THAT DIRECTION."

Although remote from his equine interests, John's involvement in family business management led him back to his first love – horses. It became the avenue to a successful commercial venture, earning fame and fortune for John, his family and the community.

In 1976, while sub-dividing a family-owned farm, he saw an opportunity to establish a home for the horses he had always craved to own. He had already bought several horses and was keeping them on a friend's property, letting his friend's children enter them in horse shows. The farm offered a more permanent arrangement and several advantages.

Although located in the country, it lay within Auburn community limits with access to city water and utilities. The farm was also near a major highway interchange, giving it an excellent business location. Thus Richland Ranch was born, which was to become a catalyst in launching Narmont's second career as a renowned breeder and show organizer as John, with his wife Sondra, became deeply involved in the highly competitive world of show horses, riding and breeding.

"I've always had a love of Palomino horses," John said, "so I started out in that direction."

It wasn't long, however, that directions changed and Richland Ranch became more diversified. Today it is heralded as one of the best modern breeding facilities in the nation, offering the finest care for horses.

Closed circuit video cameras and a highly professional staff allow a 24-hour operational facility offering breeding, training and full service care. Palominos are no longer featured and Narmont has focused his

<186>

business on Quarter Horse breeding.

Leading the pack of his champions, is Zippos Mr Good Bar, a prize-winning sire that has won nationwide acclaim for over a decade. Mr Good Bar is on the leading sire list of the American Quarter Horse Association for siring performance earning horses and has been a leading sire of money winning Western Pleasure horses and world champions at many shows, including the Quarter Horse World Show, the World Championship Paint Show and the World Championship Palomino Show.

John said Mr Good Bar has won more than $50,000 in prizes, was the top U.S. money earner in 1986 and became the leading money-earning three-year-old in 1987. Also in 1987, he became Congress Reserve Champion in the 3-Year-Old Derby. In 1988 and 89 he was the Solid Gold Futurity Champion.

In the year 2000, Zippos Mr Good Bar was inducted into the National Snaffle Bit Association Hall of Fame in both Show Horse and Breeding categories. The many times prizewinner is only the second horse in NSBA history to be inducted for both categories.

John has good reason to be proud of his business success and award winning show horses. But John has not let those accomplishments form the sum of his career goals. John continues to maintain a solid law practice while exploring other venues in addition to ranch operations. While conversing with a group of local Palomino horse exhibitors in 1981, John suggested yet another business undertaking that they all could profit from.

> "THERE'S NO REASON WHY WE CAN'T HAVE A $100,000 WEANLING PURSE FOR A SHOW RIGHT HERE IN ILLINOIS."

"You know, there's no reason why we can't have a $100,000 Weanling Purse for a show right here in Illinois," he told them.

John said they all looked at him as if he had lost his marbles, "but we soon turned that idea into reality. We formed an event called the Solid Gold Futurity, starting with a Weanling purse in 1983 of $4,000. In '84 it doubled and after several years grew to over $150,000."

John helped manage the non-profit Futurity until it finally moved from the area in the late '90s. Yet his show involvement didn't

<187>

end there. John joined forces with notable horseman Webb Parlier to promote other events. Their partnership resulted ultimately in the formation of the International Livestock Exposition, which is, in fact, the actual and legal successor to the old Chicago based International Livestock Show.

"It was a rewarding experience," John said. "I learned a great deal from many of the people I worked with...fair promotion, exhibition promotion, use of the fairgrounds, marketing and events handling."

The show continues today, earning ever-increasing appeal with an annual attendance of more than 100,000.

"It's grown in every category," John said. "We've had three shows and we've paid out over $300,000 in prizes at the 2000 show. It's tripled in size and we've added numerous events...llama show, longhorn cattle, mule and donkey congress, grade school field trips and more."

John said he doesn't look at all his ventures purely as work.

"It's work but it's also fun," he said. "I guess my positive attitude came from my parents. They always worked. My mom was a schoolteacher and my dad only attended school to the eighth grade, then he left to go to work."

"MY LAW PRACTICE REQUIRES A SEVEN-DAY WORKWEEK YET I STILL FIND TIME TO PURSUE OTHER BUSINESS IDEAS."

But his father's lack of formal education didn't slow him down. John said his father went on to build a real estate business in three states and became president of a group of banks. And like his father, John said he likes to stay busy.

"My law practice requires a seven-day workweek yet I still find time to pursue other business ideas," he said. "The ranch has been a special favorite. We breed 200 to 300 mares a year for people, shipping them in from all over the U.S. and Canada. I don't run the place day to day. I go out to the ranch weekly to inspect the physical plant, to make changes or to decide what landscaping or safety work has to be done. Sondra is at the ranch daily to handle problems and review the operation. The biggest thing I try to do is create a safe healthful environment for horses. I have a competent staff of 15 people who do just that."

John thinks the reason for his ranch success comes from his pos-

<188>

itive attitude and business philosophy.

"My theory is that it's more important what other people do and how successful they are with the offspring of my horses as opposed to what my own people and my own horses do," he said. "I'm more interested in learning that a child somewhere on a Zippos Mr Good Bar sired horse won at the Congress or World Championship Show. In other words if all our customers are being successful then that in turn will generate success for us."

John said he gains an added satisfaction from his ranch and animals that is in contrast to his work as an attorney. "Whenever I go home to the ranch, the dogs and horses are happy to see me and welcome my arrival. They never create a problem. They never get a DUI and I never get a phone call reporting that they are in jail and need to be bailed out. To me the relationship with animals and my horses in particular is often more honest and truthful than dealing with people."

> "WHENEVER I GO HOME TO THE RANCH, THE DOGS AND HORSES ARE HAPPY TO SEE ME AND WELCOME MY ARRIVAL."

<189>

GOD'S GIFT

With the exception of using one for transportation during a fishing trip, Harland Radomske had never ridden a horse until he was 40 years old. He didn't know what a bridle was – much less how to put one on a horse. And he didn't know much difference between a racehorse, a show horse and a cutting horse.

But he did have an 11-year-old daughter who wanted riding lessons. She won him over and so did the horse.

Now in his early 60s, Harland's life has taken a 180-degree turn. He has remarried, has three young children with his wife, Jody, who he married in 1986, and is an award-winning champion in the cutting horse arena.

This is his story.

<191>

"When I bought that horse for my daughter, I thought she and I could do this together, but it didn't take me but minutes until I was instantly bored with going around in circles on that horse," he said.

The next purchase for this man who knew nothing about horses was a racehorse. But that didn't hold his attention for long, either.

"I realized there's nothing much you can do [with a racehorse] except jump up and down on the sidelines," he said.

It's not as if Harland had nothing better to do. He started his own business, Venture Construction, at age 23 and built it up to become very profitable. He owned five ranches, some of which were apple orchards, some irrigation farms and another on which he lives today, which he calls Venture Farms.

> **"THERE'S NOTHING MUCH YOU CAN DO [WITH A RACEHORSE] EXCEPT JUMP UP AND DOWN ON THE SIDE-LINES."**

Why Venture?

"Well, I formed Venture Construction in 1964," he said. "And you can't answer the phone 'Radomske Construction.' So I thumbed through the dictionary and saw that one of the definitions for venture was 'a speculative business risk.' That's exactly what I was doing at age 23, so it stuck."

Still, he wasn't completely satisfied with his horses. So he chatted with the woman who taught his riding lessons, and she suggested he visit a cutting horse competition.

"It seemed like a challenge, watching them," he said. "The people were friendly, happy and seemed like they enjoyed what they were doing."

In 1982, Harland purchased his first cutting horse and began traveling around the country in his spare time to participate in weekend clinics taught by such greats as Tommy Lyons, Leon Harrell, Larry Reeder and Dick Gaines. He even bought some of the lessons through charity auctions. He also became a proud member of the National Cutting Horse Association.

He was hooked.

And it was a good time to be hooked. Cutting horses were red hot, and they could be used as a tax write-off for those in the business.

<192>

HARLAND & JODY RADOMSKE

He purchased the stallion Doc Bar Gem, which was the son of Doc Bar and about 25 mares. So he was living the dual life of a rancher and a contractor.

An intense learner, Harland soon began training and working cutting horses. He raised a brown, gelding that seemed to have potential. He sent him to a professional female trainer to be trained. He named the horse The Gemnist for two reasons: When watching this colt, he noticed it was very athletic – like a gymnast. And the colt's sire was Doc Bar Gem.

"My daughter was one of the best gymnasts in her school, so the name is tied to that, too," he said.

In 1985, he won the NCHA Futurity with The Gemnist, ridden by the second and youngest female pro rider ever to take the title. He said he left with the colt and a $264,000 check in his back pocket. Although the horse is now retired and still resides at Venture Farms, Harland said he's won more than $450,000 in competition earnings.

Harland was on a roll. Although the 1986 tax reform act made the horse industry a financial wreck for those involved, he survived and that year won the $10,000 non-pro Futurity Championships. The next year, he credits God for giving him the best gift yet: his wife, Jody.

"She's the number one thing in my life," he said. "She's younger than me but sometimes she has a hard time keeping up."

On the subject of cutting horse competitions, Harland said, "It's a true cross between a sport and an art. You've got to work at it to be good, like any sport. By the same token, it's mentally challenging, and you have to have an awareness of what's around you all at once, and you have to respond quickly.

"It's one of the ultimates in horsemanship. The horses are better broke, the timing has to be precise and no one can buy into the sport. You can't win all the time…with the elements of the cattle, horses and people all needing to come together at the right time and right seconds, you can't get that to happen all the time. You just try to increase the number of times you're good by working at it and being consistent."

> "SHE'S YOUNGER THAN ME BUT SOME-TIMES SHE HAS A HARD TIME KEEP-ING UP."

<193>

Another reason Harland is so fond of horses is that it has been a special bond for his new family. Jason, the couple's son, is a team roper and calf roper who competed in the nation high school rodeo finals after bringing home the Washington State High School Championship saddle.

Jody rides and competes as well. She was chosen for a four-person Team USA to represent the United States in the 1998 International Cutting Horse Championship in Jackson, Mississippi.

Although Harland said the younger Kyle "does not care about horses," he still has the family's competitiveness but focuses his energies in baseball, basketball and computers.

And then there's Raley Mae, the apple of Harland's eye, who has riding in her blood. Her most recent title is the Reserve Champion of the Northwest Cutting Horse Association in the junior youth 13-and-under category.

"She's a real partner," he said, beaming. "She likes to fish and hunt with me. She's likes to do everything...even to get dressed up and go to church. She is already a horsewoman."

> "SHE LIKES TO FISH AND HUNT WITH ME. SHE'S LIKES TO DO EVERY-THING."

Although Harland recently retired from the construction business, don't think for a moment that he has slowed down. The spring of 2000 brought this active competitor the Western National NCHA championship at Ogden, Utah. He now competes regularly in the northwest and has won Canadian, California and Las Vegas futurity competitions. A recent past president of the Northwest NCHA, he has since sold all of his other ranches, and recently burst a herd of 450 registered Angus bull and cattle that he built and developed.

He also stands a young stallion, The Dualler, who had the same mother as The Gemnist.

"Every one of her babies has been an outstanding individual," he said.

Harland said the family also shares the most important of bonds – a relationship with Christ.

"God is a very big part of our lives and I'm very thankful for all He's given me," he said.

<194>

HARLAND & JODY RADOMSKE

"I probably don't have a more satisfying thing than to watch my wife and little girl walk down the alleyway with their horses, hand in hand. I don't know what more a guy could want in life than that."

<195>

Shane Rux©

TRIUMPH OVER ADVERSITY

Rhonda Replogle possesses as much spirit, if not more, than the Quarter horses she owns on her ranch in Clear Springs, Maryland. At various times throughout her life, she has encountered times of personal adversity. She has discovered, however, that a fierce determination within herself and plenty of help from her friends and family has gone a long way in helping her to overcome obstacles.

The first obstacle that she had to deal with, she said, was a childhood shyness that caused her to "hide behind her parents' legs."

After her mother taught her how to ride horses at an early age, she developed a burning desire to compete in various 4-H events in her home state of Pennsylvania. It was during those shows that she found out how much she enjoyed meeting people.

"At these shows, meeting and getting to know people really made me grow as a person," Rhonda said. "Now I know people from all over the country."

> **"I DIDN'T HAVE ANY SELF-PITY, MY ATTITUDE WAS, 'I'M GOING TO BEAT THIS THING...GET OUT OF THE WAY, BECAUSE I'M COMING THROUGH.'"**

When Rhonda was a teenager, her family bought a malnourished, unbroken, shaven 2-year old mare that she named Balli Hi. After nursing the horse back to health, she worked with her and found out that she was both athletic and versatile.

On top of her talented mare, Rhonda said she won the high-point youth award with a record-setting 1181 state points. She also won the Youth Congress in the reining event and the next day she won the western pleasure event on the horse.

The same year, Rhonda said she won the seventh Congress medallion and a third place award in reining another mare named Miss India Deck.

Rhonda attended Findlay College in Ohio for two years, earning an associate degree. She joked that the professors told her it was time for her to get a job, so she took their advice and worked for Darlene Trein, a horse trainer in Newcastle, Pennsylvania, for three years. Then she worked for a man in Maryland for two years before going out on her own. She eventually returned to that same farm in Clear Springs and bought it.

When she was in her 30s, Rhonda said she was diagnosed with breast cancer. Although weakened from a radical mastectomy with reconstruction and a round of chemotherapy, she was determined to go to the American Quarter Horse Congress in Columbus, Ohio. Her father drove her, and she competed in the Miller Hunter and Saddle Futurity event.

"I didn't have any self-pity," she said. "My attitude was, 'I'm going to beat this thing...get out of the way, because I'm coming through.'"

That November she purchased Sky Blue Walker, a premium quality quarter horse that lifted her spirits even more. At the time, she realized that he could become very well known through promotion and

<198>

exposure. But, even more importantly, the horse inspired her to focus on something other than herself.

"That stallion gave me an incentive to bring myself back," she said. "It made me strive to do something instead of lying on the bed and looking at myself."

To date her cancer is in complete remission.

The versatile Rhonda still competes in a wide variety of events, including halter, all-around in western and English riding, reining, youth and amateur. In 2000, she won four Justin rookie-of-the-year awards.

Along with her horse breeding, training and showing, she judges horse shows for the Pinto Horse Association, the Buckskin Association and the National Snaffle Bit Association.

At her ranch she also teaches small groups of teen-age girls and boys to ride and show horses at the Youth World Congress. Although their training takes time and a great deal of patience, she finds it rewarding.

"Watching the kids walk up to the platform to receive their awards is my natural high," she said.

Rhonda said that even though she has to start at "square one" with some of the youth, she does not mind as long as they have the desire to learn.

"If mom and dad try to make them take lessons, it won't work," she said.

Rhonda recalled that one girl with whom she worked had taken ballet, piano, and jazz lessons, but she did not like any of those activities. On a whim, she cashed in a "free riding lesson" coupon donated by Rhonda to benefit the Cystic Fibrosis Association. She enjoyed the lesson so much that she has been a student for eight years and has even won a national title.

> "IF MOM AND DAD TRY TO MAKE THEM TAKE LESSONS, IT WON'T WORK."

"This is the only thing the child has liked to do," Rhonda said. "Her family has gone from owning one horse to buying a big dually truck with a 38-foot horse trailer."

According to Rhonda, there's something for everyone when it comes to showing horses. Some of her students enjoy both the Western

<199>

pleasure riding and English riding events. Others want to be perfectionists at only one type of event. One man who has been her customer for seven years had back surgery and was unable to ride. His way of continuing in the horse business was to participate in the halter horse event, which allowed him to show horses without riding them.

Rhonda said she also enjoys the challenge of training individual horses, because she tries to understand how they think. Sometimes it takes her a couple of days to figure an individual horse out, but said she usually she knows the horse's mind right away. Even though some horses try to play "head games" with her, she said that with most horses, "what you see is what you get."

"Everyone tries to make horse training a physical game," she said. "They muscle horses into doing things. To me, it's more of a mental game. I have to figure out what the horses like and dislike. Like people, they have their own 'pet peeves'. There's no sense making them do something. The horses won't like their job, and they'll hate to come out every day. It's like working at McDonald restaurant instead of doing what you really want to do."

> "EVERYONE TRIES TO MAKE HORSE TRAINING A PHYSICAL GAME. THEY MUSCLE HORSES INTO DOING THINGS."

Rhonda said that she has learned discipline and living on a strict schedule from her classes in horsemanship, patterns and reining. Even though she tries to take time off from her busy life on the ranch, she rarely gets a chance. She does get to travel to various places, however, when she is judging a show or taking her students to compete in the annual youth competitions.

The adversities of daily life that challenge the courageous woman never give her a break either. During her drive home from the Youth World Congress in 2000, she stopped to check her horses. After she fed them and put the grain buckets back in the trailer, she accidentally slid down the ramp and fractured her ankle in two places.

Undaunted, she did some of her daily work on crutches. For the most part, however, she was forced to sit at her desk and do paperwork with her foot "propped up with ice on it." She was grateful for the amateurs and her students who helped her with the chores.

<200>

RHONDA REPLOGLE

"If someone gets injured, people come together from across the country and help him out," she said. "If your trailer breaks down, another horse person is willing to stop and help you. The horse-raising industry is like one big, happy family."

Rhonda's mother, who has helped her every day in the barn since she started her own business, was also of great assistance to her. She said she is thankful that her parents, Ralph and Nancy, were willing to sacrifice everything for her so she could pursue her dream.

In October of 1999, her father passed away, leaving Rhonda and her mother.

"He was a great person who was both easygoing and hard-working," she said.

> "THE HORSE-RAISING INDUSTRY IS LIKE ONE BIG, HAPPY FAMILY."

<201>

ERNEST RICCO

TENACIOUS LOVE

Ernest Ricco was made of stern stuff. And that explains in part how his daughter, Hedy Voigt, and son-in-law, Pat Voigt, have had the amazing tenacity and ability to run a ranch, raise children and take care of ailing parents.

Hedy's mother has Alzheimer's and her late husband had Parkinson's disease.

"We pretty much work from daylight to dark," she said, but added that it's a labor of love because she has adored animals from her earliest days.

Born October 10, 1908, Ernest Ricco, Jr., died in his sleep on April 24, 2000, after a hard-fought battle with Parkinson's disease. He was the son of Ernest Ricco, Sr., and Annie Amacher, who came to the

<203>

United States from Europe in 1888 (they spoke very little English).

In 1897, they started farming on 50 acres of land just off Dixie Creek Road, four miles from Prairie City, Oregon.

"IT WAS THE AMERICAN DREAM. I DON'T THINK YOU CAN DO THAT NOW."

"Dad was one of seven children," Hedy said. "The family stayed together until all of them had their own ranches in the area. They didn't have much when they came to this country.

"But horses were very important to the Ricco family. They used horses for transportation, for working the fields, mowing hay, raking hay, stacking it. They didn't have any motorized vehicles in the very beginning."

Thanks to her father's foresight, Ricco Ranch became the first commercial turkey breeder in Oregon, with 7,000 turkeys.

"Then they branched out, and managed to clear $10,000, which would be like $100,000 today," Hedy said. "That's when the boys started farming on their own."

Around those parts, Ernest Ricco was also known as an innovative man.

"He wasn't afraid to try anything new, which was why he had the first turkey farm in Oregon," Hedy said. "At the time they still mowed hay with the horses. I still remember as a little girl, plowing ditches with a team. I wouldn't miss a day out there."

She recalled with a smile that her father was also "kind of stubborn in ways. He had tractors, but he thought that no tractor could dig a ditch like that hand plow and team."

She smiled at a poignant memory and added, "I would wrap my arms in the harness and I'd fall asleep. I'd cry because when Dad came to get me, I didn't want to get off."

She also remembers her dad as "a little man with lots of grit. He would tackle any project that needed to be done."

Today, she and Pat still live on the home place where the Riccos started out.

"We have water in the spring, but in recent years we've had problems with forest fires," she said. "That seven-mile ditch, that many said couldn't be done, has really helped. Dad also tried to make a glacier. He wanted to

<204>

freeze a wall of water in high country so it would run off for irrigating. But he never got it to completion. I think it would have worked."

Hedy said her father was also a trailblazer in using artificial insemination (AI), which was considered absolutely revolutionary when he first tried it.

"When we first got into AI," she said, "people thought we were totally nuts. Dad went to Illinois and took this class on artificial insemination. My uncle had a fit and asked, 'What are you going to do next?'

"Dad came back from Illinois and bred a few cows…and then he talked me into going to take a class. I was the only girl in there. The instructor looked at me and I looked at him. And I could tell he was thinking, 'Here's this gal. Well, I can't wait till she gets fertilizer all over her."

Hedy laughed and said, "He and I turned out to be the best of friends…and we joke about it now. I've got too much of my father in me. It wasn't a pleasant job, but I wasn't giving up."

She said that when they were simply considering using AI, her father asked her if she thought they could do it.

"I told him that I felt confident that we could," she said, "but what if we can't? So he went to the man who taught us, and said, 'Well, Stan, if I offered you $100 a day to come down and help us out…'"

And he did.

"My husband also took a class," Heddy said, "and he's faster at it so we gave him the job. AI was a revolutionary move for us. It increased productivity greatly."

Her father's next step was traveling to Germany to view firsthand the beautiful Simmental cattle.

"We went there and we were so impressed that we bred 400 cows to Simmental," she said. "Our calves increased 75 to 100 pounds."

> "I COULD TELL HE WAS THINKING, WELL, I CAN'T WAIT TILL SHE GETS FERTIL- IZER ALL OVER HER."

Ricco Ranch then experimented with other breeds such as Limousin, Charolais, Main Anjou, Beef Brown Swiss and Angus. Their newest cross with Braunvieh bulls excited Hedy, who "couldn't wait until the calves hit the ground in the spring of 2001."

What she remembers most about her father was that "He was

< 205 >

honest and took people at their word. A handshake was the way you did business."

She added, "He was born out here in the family blacksmith shop…and he was married here at the home place…and he died here, which was his wish."

Hedy is every bit as much an animal lover as her dad. And she was fortunate to marry a man who shares her interests.

"I have a tremendous husband," she said. She and Pat were high-school sweethearts who married after college in 1973.

"My husband didn't grow up on a ranch, but he worked on them," she said. "We had the same goals. We both wanted a ranch. And like dad would always say, 'Set your pegs and drive to 'em.'

"Growing up, horses were all I cared about. They were my favorite. Dogs were second, cats third…and lambs, you had to throw them in there, too."

Hedy said the cattle business has its ups and downs.

"Some years you're lucky to break even, and some years, you do well," she said. "If you don't love it or you don't want to work 24 hours a day, don't get into it. During calving season, we never leave the cows alone. Someone's with them around the clock."

> "HE WAS BORN OUT HERE IN THE FAMILY BLACKSMITH SHOP, MARRIED HERE AND DIED HERE."

One of Ernest Ricco's rules of ranching still prevails at Ricco Ranch today.

"He taught us to feed the animals before we feed ourselves," Hedy said. "To this day, that's the way I am."

Ernest Ricco, passing on the torch to Hedy's son, called him and made him promise to take care of the family ranch.

"It was a very emotional time," she said. "My son was the pride and joy of my father."

She and Pat have raised their children on the Ricco Ranch near Prairie City, which has a population of 1,000.

"Let's put it this way, " she said. " We don't have an electronic stop sign, and I drove 300 miles to have my children in Portland."

The Voigts' daughter, Riccola, will graduate high school in 2002, has completed modeling school and reached the finals of a New York competition. She is considering Texas colleges, and perhaps a career in law.

Hedy said their son, Jason, in his 20s, is a logger and loves it.

"From the time he was born, he knew what he wanted to do," she said. "He has a brand-new pickup and a John Deere tractor and wants an alfalfa farm."

The century-old Ricco Ranch has 300 breeding cows.

"To work the ranch we use Blazers, which are tough little horses," Hedy said. "They're smart and make an excellent ranch horse. We have hills and rocks, and those horses just won't quit. My daughter did a seminar with the breeder when she was only four. He said, 'Buy one of these and we'll train it together.' He had her riding it within three hours."

> "TO WORK THE RANCH WE USE BLAZERS, WHICH ARE TOUGH LITTLE HORSES."

While Riccola likes horses, Jason has "always been more into machinery."

Her father's last gifts to the kids were saddles he had made for both of them. As for Hedy, she doesn't have to look far for sentimental reminders of her dad.

"I go in that barn and he's with me...the harnesses, the bridles he used," he used. "I pick up one of those things, and he's there."

Boasting a 59-year marriage before his death, Hedy said Ernest Ricco felt qualified to offer tips on relationships.

She smiled and said, "He'd say you ought to get your divorce before you get married. In other words, have things all lined up beforehand."

"At a wedding, he'd tell a bride and groom that the first 50 years are the hardest. And then he would tell them that his best advice was to "have a big fight first off so you can see who's boss."

Two other Ernest Ricco adages: Avoid bad people like the plague. And try to find some fun in everything you do.

"While irrigating he would point out bird nests and we would gather wildflowers," Hedy said. "He put the Farmer's Creed in the family Bible because it described the simple, honest way he lived his life."

The hospitality, the lessons of equality – Hedy said these are things that come to mind when she thinks of her father.

"I think what my father put together is pretty amazing."

<207>

PUTTING DOWN ROOTS

T homas Saunders' family has been on the same ranch outside Weatherford, Texas since 1934. He grew up as a cowboy on the acres of pastureland near Lipan and Brock.

"We're cow people in cow country, and we ride cow horses, too," Saunders said. "My uncle had the World Champion Cutting Horse Stallion in 1957, a horse named King's Pistol."

Saunders pursues his heritage as a cattleman with a passion for the land and the creatures that live on it.

The Saunders Cattle Company is primarily a ranching business, but Thomas started riding outside horses for extra pocket money.

"It's just been me," he said. "I started that when I was 16 or 17 years old and have been doing it ever since."

< 2 0 9 >

That industrious enterprise has turned into Saunders Ranch Horse Training where the owner and his crew ride and break horses for the public.

> "WE GET SOME THOROUGHBREDS TO BREAK AND SOME THAT ARE GOING TO THE TRACK TO RUN."

"We ride anywhere from 100 to 125 horses a year," he said. "We break a lot of outside horses. Quarter horses, that's what we like."

Saunders said that for the ranching business the Quarter bred horse is best suited for the work.

"We like a horse that's ideally 15 hands to 15 one or two and weighs about 1,100 to 1,300 pounds," he said. "They've got stamina to carry you all day and they have cow working instincts."

For his riding business, it's a different story – depending on what his hands are given. They ride many different breeds, but most often they get Quarter horses.

"We get some thoroughbreds to break and some that are going to the track to run," he said.

They've also ridden Tennessee Walkers and even mules. Saunders said breaking a mule is an interesting experience. But regardless of preference, in his cattle business the horses are essential.

"We use the horses every day," he said. "We gather stock with them, drag calves when we're branding and we sort cattle with them."

Whatever Saunders and his crew do when working with the cattle, they do from atop a horse. A growing trend in the industry has been to use three-wheelers, but Saunders has strong feelings about that.

"We don't use three-wheelers, we don't condone it and we don't hang around anybody that does," he said. "We're cow people in cow country, and we're going to ride cow horses, too."

In his 20 plus years of experience in riding horses for the public and nearly 40 years of living on a ranch, Saunders found it difficult to single out one horse that was more special than the others. He said each one is different, but they're all special.

"We've got several different horses that certain special things stick out in my mind about each and every one of them." He said. "There's just some of them that are special, something that we did together than sticks out in my mind."

< 2 1 0 >

Each horse teaches him something different, he said, and each horse needs individualized attention so you can learn his or her way of understanding and communicating. Some need to go faster, some need to go slower and some require more attention on certain lessons and less on others.

"You learn to communicate with them, you learn different things, what it takes to break a horse down or to go ahead and communicate with it," he said. "Sometimes you keep banging your head against the wall trying to get this horse to respond to one certain thing. Sometimes it's just right there in front of you and you've just been working around it from the beginning, and then it slaps you in the face. You can take a different angle toward a colt that you might not have done with the one right before."

Saunders said much of what he has learned working with the horses is applicable to working with people.

"It teaches you a lot of things you can use with people."

Drought conditions in Texas over the years have been hard on Saunders and his stock.

"It [drought] hasn't completely annihilated us yet, but it's certainly given us limitations and restrictions that we have to live under on a day-to-day basis that we wouldn't ordinarily do if we'd had plenty of water and moisture both."

To cope with the excessive summer heat and dry conditions, the rancher moves the cattle on a regular basis. His cattle are located in various places – some of which are 60 miles away from headquarters. The cowboys check on them once or twice a week. The cattle business, Saunders reiterated, is an every day responsibility.

"We're constantly having to monitor our water resources," he said. "We want to know if something's not going right. If they're not performing the way they should because the grass is dry and there's not any water, then we want to be on top of things quickly enough to move them to a different place or make adjustments as we go.

"That's what we do as cowboys. We constantly monitor stock and

> "IT [DROUGHT] HASN'T COMPLETELY ANNIHILATED US YET, BUT IT'S CERTAINLY GIVEN US LIMITATIONS AND RESTRICTIONS."

<211>

try to be good stewards of the land. Right now it's really, really hard to do. The Lord gives us moisture and it's our job to use that moisture and manage this grass to the best of its potential."

Saunders said he constantly monitors conditions and makes adjustments to care for the cattle and the horses. For example, when the grass gets too dry or too short in one area the cattle have to be moved or they will start to show that there is a lack of feed.

"They'll get thin, they won't perform as well, they might not want to breed, they might not produce as much milk as they need to for that calf," he said.

A typical day on his ranch begins at 5:30 a.m. with the feeding of the horses.

"We start catching horses around six o'clock, saddle them and getting ready to go do our daily business," he said. "And we try to be headed to wherever we're headed to no later than six-thirty."

The morning is spent checking on the cattle and moving them if necessary. In the scorching Texas summer heat, an attempt is made to finish most of the work in the pasture by noon. In the afternoon it's barn chores and other mainte-

> A TYPICAL DAY ON HIS RANCH BEGINS AT 5:30 A.M. WITH THE FEEDING OF THE HORSES.

nance chores. When the mercury cruises past the 100-degree mark, there's an effort to stick close to the barn and the shade. It's healthier for humans as well as the horses.

"We'll catch a colt, tie him in the shade up there, pick his feet up, brush on him, teach him to ground tie, and do those kinds of things," he said.

Ground tying is a lesson the horses must learn. Saunders describes it as teaching the horse to stay put.

"If you dropped your bridle reins and you're in the middle of a pasture, and that horse is taught to ground tie, he won't move from where you dropped the reins on him," he said.

In the evening, colts are ridden that weren't used that morning. The horses, he said, need consistent riding and training and different horses require different time lengths for training.

"Usually we try to have a green horse standing to be saddled, standing to be gotten on, and to have respect for a bit within 30 days," he said. "It takes a while."

Saunders uses what he calls the "horsemanship method" to work with his charges.

"It's just the good old gentle horsemanship method, the Thomas Saunders method, the John Ed Rogers method, the Calvin Wills method," he said.

The rancher said he and his crew take everything they know and approach the horse. Each horse will require something a little different to communicate.

With his experience and heritage, Thomas Saunders works every day to be a good steward. Early mornings and blazing afternoons may present daily challenges and new issues, but making little adjustments as he goes along is a way of life for this cattle and horseman. That's what Cowboys do.

> EACH HORSE WILL REQUIRE SOMETHING A LITTLE DIFFERENT TO COMMUNICATE.

<213>

DOUG & SUE SCHEMBRI

DECADES OF HORSE RAISING

When Doug Schembri was in his teens he dreamed of riding a motorcycle on the Florida highways. His mother, however, refused to let him have one because she felt it was too dangerous. She decided that he should have a horse instead. Little did Doug know at the time that he would soon make his living out of his newfound passion for horses.

An extra benefit was discovering that his high school sweetheart, Sue, loved horses too. She had saved up her lunch money to buy a horse from a friend who owned them.

"It was a wild and crazy old horse that was some 20 odd years old…and he tried to run away from me every time I was going to get on him," Sue recalled, laughing.

<215>

Doug and Sue met at a skating rink and became good friends, enjoying social outings together. They went to many horse shows and sales and Doug eventually added five more horses to his stable.

During the Vietnam War Doug was drafted into the Army but got stationed in Anchorage, Alaska, because of his "sole-surviving son" status. Doug and Sue were married during that time and their honeymoon involved hauling two of their horses on a 1300-mile frozen stretch of Alaskan highway to their destination. One of the passengers in the trailer was Sue's 20-year-old horse, which she dared not leave in Florida "because he was too old and a non-sweater."

"IT TOOK "TIME, COMMON SENSE, AND UNDERSTANDING OF ANIMALS TO MAKE IT WORK."

When they returned to their home in Sarasota after Doug's stint in the Army, the horse died.

Doug became a blacksmith after a two-year apprenticeship and shoed horses for seven years. He built up a good clientele and eventually got interested in showing horses. During that time Sue took several courses on horse breeding – and over the years, they acquired the ability and experience to handle and show horses. According to Sue, it took "time, common sense, and understanding of animals to make it work."

Today Doug and Sue own Char-O-Lot Ranch, a 70-acre spread in Myakka City, which is on the outskirts of Sarasota. They have "about 150 stalls" and primarily mainly house Appaloosas, along with some Quarter horses. Their specialty is breeding halter horses for sale.

Married since 1972, Doug and Sue said they owe their happiness to that solid friendship they developed in high school.

"You have to be good friends to stick together," Sue said. "If you aren't your relationship is just a big hot flash that doesn't last."

The Schembri ranch is largely a family operation. Jennifer, a daughter born in 1974, is an attorney in Sarasota who also shows horses. Sue said Jennifer is capable of running every part of the business if she and Doug are gone for some reason.

And Sean, a son born in 1987, works every day until 1 p.m. during summer months when not in school, feeding the mares and help-

<216>

ing Doug with the ponies.

"Raising horses has helped keep our family close together," Doug said. "With the horse business, Sue and I are here when Sean comes home from school. I don't have to be at a job…I'm right here for him."

Doug and Sue have noticed that growing the family business has been good for both of the children because it has kept them occupied and has given them goals.

"The best thing about children working with horses is that it gives them something to work for and teaches them some responsibility," Sue said. "No matter what they choose to do later in life, they'll always have that to take with them."

Sean is a diabetic and Sue said that by working with the horses he benefits in the area of his self-esteem. She thinks the horse industry encourages him to feel better about himself by placing him in a division where he can make progress showing his horse.

For the Schembri family traveling to horse shows in different states is like a family vacation. They stay in hotels, eat out at restaurants and enjoy socializing with longtime friends they have not seen for a while at the shows. Even though they work hard preparing their horses and showing them, they enjoy what they are doing.

"We're making a good living doing our hobby," Doug said. "We've been lucky making it work, because it can be a tough business."

> "WE'RE MAKING A GOOD LIVING DOING OUR HOBBY."

The Schembris do their own breeding, raise their stallions and build their own show programs. They operate on a strict daily schedule, regulating the feeding times of the horses, which usually only vary by about 20 minutes. On the show circuit the horses get their bed changed five times a day and are pampered with a special grooming process before being presented in front of the judges.

Doug and Sue also have to ensure the safety of the horses when they travel in the trailer. They have to use the right equipment and facilities to keep them healthy and bright for the show day.

Despite their meticulous planning, however, any number of problems can and do occur. At times they have to deal with a horse get-

<217>

ting sick, banging its legs into the sides of the trailer, stumbling on something or developing body sores.

"A show horse is not like a car that you can park in a garage, shut the door, come out the next week and everything is the same," Doug said. "You have to take care of them 24 hours a day."

Even though Doug and Sue have cultivated a "farmer's mentality" when it comes to the financial aspects of the horse-raising business, they still find it difficult to not get emotionally attached to their horses.

"Every year, we have 30 to 40 babies," Sue said. "We always have a few that don't make it. We do everything in our power to save them, but sometimes it isn't meant to be. It's taken me a long time to get over that, but it is something I had to deal with."

Unlike many horse breeders, however, the Schembris don't cull horses when they get older. They currently house and pasture a dozen retired geldings that their children showed when they were younger.

Doug and Sue enjoy facing the challenges of each day. Doug likes the marketing aspects of the business and the effort it takes to keep customers coming back over the years.

"WE'VE LEARNED TO ROLL WITH THE PUNCHES IN THE HORSE BUSINESS."

"People in this country do not have to have a horse," Doug said. "We market the product so that people can enjoy it and have fun. Some of them can make money out of it, but a lot of them can't. We want them back after they show one. We've got to take care of them so that when they want the next one, they'll come back to us."

Sue delights in developing the potential of each horse and breeding in particular because "it's a challenge getting mares to foal." She also enjoys meeting new people every day from all over the country.

"We've learned to roll with the punches in the horse business," Sue said. "Some good things, as well as bad things, happen. With our clients, when something bad happens to their horse, it's like the end of the world. But every day is different, and you have to go with the flow. You live with what God gives you, and then you go on."

<218>

<219>

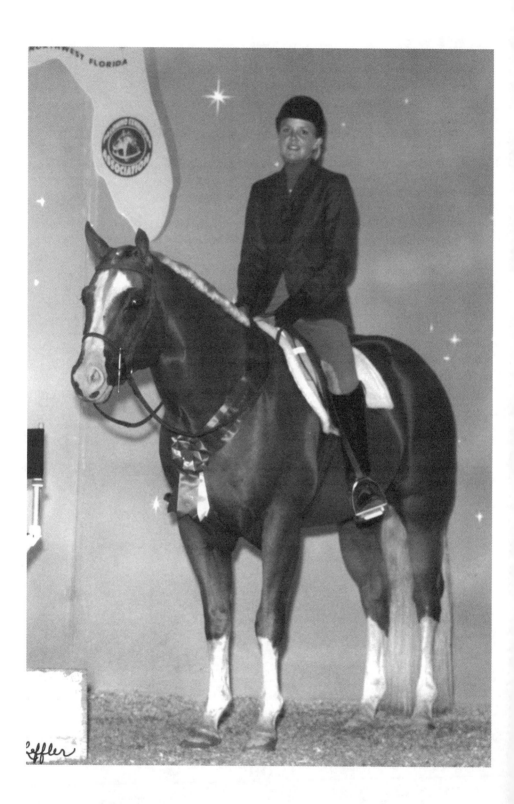

HORSES AND THE SPIRIT

Mythology is filled with tales of enchanted horses and none are more fascinating than that of Pegasus and the Unicorn. These mystical equine creatures have cast a spell over young and old readers over the centuries. They portray the horse as the noblest and most steadfast of animals, serving man and often saving him from his enemies.

No wonder then that the horse has inspired mankind throughout history. That is, perhaps, why we are so often awe-struck with the almost magical sense of strength and endurance that the horse brings to the animal kingdom.

The beauty and grace of horses can also lead us to a better understanding of God and the gifts of nature. It is difficult to deny our cre-

< 2 2 1 >

ator when we view the majesty of the horse and all the other creatures that populate our planet.

So it was for Benham and Louise Stewart, who recognized in the horse a marvelous treasure of creation.

Benham and Louise have always recognized the Holy Spirit in nature. Their venture into the kingdom of horses has been not only a vocation, but also a ministry that has helped them to bond more closely with other humans and other animals. Their commercial undertaking has, indeed, become so spiritually centered that it bears the additional marks of a service to our Creator.

THEIRS IS ALSO A STORYBOOK ROMANCE THAT BEGAN IN CHILD-HOOD.

Theirs is also a storybook romance that began in childhood. They rode horses together as young-sters, through high school and beyond. And though they dated other people, both approved of the people each dated.

So one day by mutual agreement they concluded that since they were so comfortable being together that they should marry within five years. The marriage came to be and bore fruit in ways the couple could not at the time imagine.

Benham's early experience with horses occurred well before his marriage to Louise. He lived with his family on five acres of land in Macon, Georgia. His father was a doctor who, when Benham was four, gave his son a pony. The boy and the pony soon became steadfast com-panions. He quickly learned to ride him and cared for him as a prized possession.

"My daddy thought that would be the end of it," Benham said. "But we soon went from owning a pony to a horse, then two horses, and then began swapping and trading horses."

Thus began Benham's early love of horses.

"I rode a horse everywhere around town," he remembered. "It was common for me to go to a store or to my daddy's office and hitch my horse to a parking meter."

The rest of Benham's life was more normal. He attended local schools, joined the Mulberry Methodist Church and graduated from a local college.

He began a more serious involvement in the equine arena when

<222>

BENHAM & LOUISE STEWART

he discovered a celebrity horse living in his hometown of Macon. The president of local Wesleyan College owned a Palomino stallion named Flash Trigger, which was the offspring of Trigger, the famed wonder horse featured in Roy Rogers' western movies.

Benham rode the horse whenever possible and, when the college president prepared to leave Macon, bought Flash Trigger for his own.

By then he had moved his horse breeding activities to the family farmlands know as Singing Pines Plantation. The farm was located near Glenwood, Georgia and was comprised of several thousand acres of prime timber and cattle grazing land. The plantation was given its name by his grandfather.

"He called it Singing Pines" Benham said, "because of the musical sound the wind made blowing through the pine trees behind the old homesite."

Six generations of the Stewart family have made the plantation the outstanding holding it is today. The property's major revenue originally came from the sale of naval stores, including turpentine and other timber byproducts. Farming and cattle were soon introduced, but when Benham became involved horse breeding began in earnest.

Louise had always dreamed of living on a horse ranch, so when the two were married she found a haven in Singing Pines. Together she and Benham established their business, raised a family and took an active role in church activities.

Their son and daughter, Butch and Lulu, have contributed their talents to the family undertaking, winning numerous competitions and awards in horsemanship. The family continues in those pursuits today, concentrating first on their central relationship with the Holy Spirit and secondarily with their business undertakings in Palomino and Quarter horse breeding.

These pursuits have led the family not only to business success, but also to a greater communion with the many friends and associates that have affected their lives.

The Palomino Horse Breeding Association (PHBA) champi-

> SIX GENERATIONS OF THE STEWART FAMILY HAVE MADE THE PLANTATION THE OUTSTANDING HOLDING IT IS TODAY.

<223>

onships earned by Singing Pines progeny are legend. Together they have accounted for six Reserve World Champions, seven third places, and third overall high point youth 14-18 and the Reserve Golden horse award. The awards list doesn't end there. The American Quarter Horse Association (AQHA) has also bestowed numerous titles on the star performers from Singing Pines. Renowned prize-winning horses include Skips My Golden Star, Starpions Lil Lady, Starpions Gold, Skippin N Stars and Skips Royal Star - - all having earned a lengthy list of prizes.

Famous people have come to own many of the 'stars' from Singing Pines. Undefeated boxing champion and Olympic Silver Medal winner, Roy Jones, Jr., also an avid horseman, bought the prize-winning stallion, Aerostars.

"The fame of the horses and their owners, however, cannot over-shadow the excellence of the dedicated trainers and associates we have known through the years," Benham said. "We owe a great debt for the friendship and charity of those who have helped us achieve our goals."

And he doesn't forget the greatest gift he and his family have been awarded.

"WE COULD NOT HAVE GOTTEN THIS FAR IF THE GOOD LORD HAD NOT BLESSED US."

"We could not have gotten this far if the good Lord had not blessed us with these truly versatile horses. They have not ceased to amaze us with their versatility, good minds, and good looks," he said. "The breeding program at singing Pines has developed beyond our expectations. We invite everyone to come and see the future stars in our pasture and those already going under saddle."

Therein lies the real success story behind singing Pines Plantation – man and animal working together in a trusting relationship that has led to great material and spiritual rewards. The Stewarts' attest to their success only as it relates to their faith and the fruits of the Holy Spirit. They believe that the success achieved is not theirs but rather belongs to God. They focus all their undertakings within the framework of their church involvement, their local ministries and missionary work.

"It's the Christian setting in which we live that has most influenced us from our beginnings until now," Benham said. "Just as a plan-

<224>

tation is multifaceted, so are our horses and the people at Singing Pines. Yet it is to God, that we give the glory for everything."

<225>

ALL IN THE FAMILY

F orty years ago newlyweds Henry and Ann Tien bought a spread outside their tiny hometown of Prairie View, Kansas to farm and ranch, and "built it up from scratch." After a period of time the Tiens realized they needed more room.

They became friends of some people who owned part of the historic Gudgel Simpson ranch, which was home to some of the best Hereford cattle in the world during the early 1900s, including the legendary bull, Prince Domino. Their friends did not have any children to inherit their farm, so they gave Henry and Ann a long-term lease on the land in 1972.

In 1973 Henry took his two oldest sons, Scott and Curtis, who were 9 and 10 years old at the time, to the annual production sale at

< 227 >

the T-Cross Ranch in Colorado Springs for the purpose of buying his first registered Quarter horse. Little did he know that he would soon be bidding against the famous Western actor John Wayne for the same horse. Wayne outlasted Henry, however, and got the final bid on the young mare.

Fortunately, Henry did not go home empty-handed. He ended up buying a two-year-old mare name Peace Cross, who was a daughter of the well-known sire, Tee Cross, and out of a Poco Pico daughter.

THE HORSE TURNED OUT TO BE A VERY INTELLIGENT AND ATHLETIC STALLION.

"She was a really nice looking mare and we were fortunate that we were able to raise a couple of fillies out of her before she died at the age of 10," Henry said.

In the late '70s Henry started breeding a few mares every year to Duane Walker's popular stallion, Jackie Bee, at Canton, Kansas. Henry kept the four best mares that he raised for his boys to show in 4-H competition. After their years in 4-H were over, Henry decided to purchase his own stallion in 1990 to breed their mares that had become a part of the family through the years. He decided on a cutting bred stallion named One Big Hotrodder, who was a grandson of Colonel Freckles and Rondo Leo.

In 1994 Henry and his two youngest sons, Steven and Kent, attended the fall production sale of Howard Pitzer, a renowned Quarter Horse breeder who has raised more AQHA champions than anyone in the breed. They bought Two Id Seek Jack, a 10-week-old red road stud colt who was a grandson of the great Two Eyed Jack. Steven said that the horse turned out to be a very intelligent and athletic stallion with a great disposition.

"That's why we breed most of our mares to him," Henry said. "We have started riding his first colts in the past year and they seem to have a lot of his same good qualities and ability, so we are really excited about his future as a sire."

The Tiens, however, give much of the credit to the man who has trained and shown Two Id Sweet Jack, Jim Brickman, who is a grandson of Pitzer. Throughout 1999 and 2000, Brickman has been showing the stallion at AQHA shows in Nebraska and the surrounding

<228>

states. One particular show that stands out, according to the Tiens, was the 2000 Pre Denver Circuit held in Denver, Colorado during January 2000.

"There were five shows held in three days and our horse won four firsts and a second in calf roping," Kent said. "He picked up 38 AQHA points in heading, heeling, and calf roping. Dad and I were able to go to the shows, so we really enjoyed that. He is qualified to compete in all three roping events at the 2000 AQHA World Show, which is held in Oklahoma City, Oklahoma every November.

The Tien family also trains some of their horses to assist with their cattle operation, using techniques that build a trusting relationship.

"When a horse understands what you want it to do, they'll work for you and try to do whatever you ask. Once we get them going well, we get them around cattle and start using them out in the pastures," Steven said.

He also said that horses have taught him patience and discipline. Whenever he trains a young horse, he starts to work it in a round pen and gets the horse to listen to him. After he establishes mutual trust between himself and the horse, Steven saddles the animal and goes for the first ride.

"The horse knows I'm not going to hurt him because I take my time," Steven said.

Over the years, Henry and his sons have turned their spread into a profitable horse-breeding program, a cattle raising operation, and a diversified farm on which they grow wheat, corn, and feed for the livestock. Their breeding season takes up a great deal of their time during the spring and early summer. They ride their horses throughout their pastures checking the cattle in the summer and rounding them up in fall. Planting and harvesting the crops and working the ground also keeps the Tiens busy from April until late October.

"WHEN A HORSE UNDERSTANDS WHAT YOU WANT IT TO DO, THEY'LL WORK FOR YOU."

Henry has passed down the legacy of a solid work ethic from his farming parents down to his sons, along with a high standard for maintaining their farmland.

"We need to leave the land in better condition when we leave this world than when we first got it," Henry said. "It takes a lot of hard work and long hours to make an operation successful."

The Tiens cherish the familial closeness they have developed from working side-by-side everyday for years. No one has an assigned chore, but they all do a little bit of everything, and work where they're needed.

"Working together in a family is a give and take situation," Henry said. "You have to work at trying to get along. If everyone is stubborn, it won't work."

Steven and Kent both still work on the farm. Kent, 28, is unmarried. His brother Steven, 31, is married and has a 4-year-old son, Aaron and a 2-year-old daughter, Sierra. Aaron likes to feed the horses, and frequently rides with his cousins when they visit. Because of her young age, Sierra rides with her father or her mother, Jaime.

Curtis, 35, has a small farm in Kentucky, but he still has mares on the Kansas ranch. He works as a welding supervisor for Chicago Bridge and Iron, a worldwide steel-manufacturing firm.

> "YOU HAVE TO WORK AT TRYING TO GET ALONG. IF EVERYONE IS STUBBORN, IT WON'T WORK."

Scott, 36, works at machine shop in Norton, Kansas, which is near Prairie View, but he often brings his children out to the farm to ride his horses. His 7- and 8-year-old sons are eager to participate soon in 4-H competition.

"My grandkids love roping the steer's head that's stuck in a bale of straw," Henry laughed and said, referring to their practice with a roping dummy.

Henry recalled how well his sons competed at the 4-H shows.

"They benefited from the shows a lot," he said. "It was something we all enjoyed together as a family. Parents have got to do a few things with their kids, and that's what we did."

When Steven was 7 years old, he won a belt buckle for his reserve champion yearling filly in 4-H. The victory inspired him to think about a career in horse raising.

"I think that lit the fire a little bit," he said.

<230>

THE TIENS

Most recently, Kent and Steven have started team roping at some local arenas owned by friends. They are both looking forward to continuing this hobby in the future, especially when they start using their horse, Two Id Sweet Jack, after his show career is over.

On Sundays, the Tiens attend a small Christian Reformed church in the country. Henry is grateful to God for seeing him through the tough times on the farm.

"THERE'S A REASON FOR EVERYTHING THAT COMES ALONG IN YOUR LIFE."

"If you have faith in God, you realize there's a reason for everything that comes along in your life," Henry said. "You benefit from the trails in life."

< 2 3 1 >

THE MAKING OF A WINNER

E ven when you love what you do there will be times of self-doubt.

But don't let that keep you down, says Jim Watts, a cutting horseman from Seguin, Texas.

"I'm living out my dream right now," said Watts from his and wife Dee Ann's 35-acre Quarter horse ranch nestled in the Hill Country, where they've lived for the past two years. "I've asked for this dream, and I have it."

Watts breeds, trains and shows cutting horses. His client list stretches from Louisiana to California and across Texas. It includes ranchers, attorneys, doctors, real estate professionals, housewives, a car dealer and even a stunt pilot. He has about 25 horses in training at any

<233>

given time and keeps 50 to 60 head on the ranch, including brood mares with babies. The premier stallion standing at the ranch is Instant Cash 595, a 5-year-old whose winnings top $70,000.

And as a trainer, Watts is in high demand: "We have a small waiting list for people, and that's a good feeling," he said.

Things look pretty bright from the hilltop ranch, where the view stretches as far as the lights of San Antonio, New Braunfels and San Marcos.

"It's a gorgeous view up on this hill. It's what I've wanted all my life, and I finally found it."

> "IT'S WHAT I'VE WANTED ALL MY LIFE, AND I FINALLY FOUND IT."

But hilltop outlooks can get cloudy and dreams may leave room for difficult days when even the pros question their abilities.

After the first half of the year 2000, Watts thought he was in "kind of in a slump," he said in his upbeat voice and unmistakable Texas twang. "I wasn't winning much. I felt like my showing was going downhill."

But Watts' tight circle of support – family, clients and colleagues – spurred him on.

"They told me to keep my head up and keep showing," he said.

So he backed up and regrouped by taking a trip to a friend's ranch near Weatherford, where they rode together. His showmanship seemed to improve, everything started to click and things started to look better. And better. And better.

Until that point, Watts had only one horse qualified for the 2000 American Quarter Horse Association World Championship Finals. He soon added another three to the winning herd.

His victories seem contagious. One of his clients made the finals in the Summer Spectacular – marking her first finals showing.

"It was just as big a moment for me as it was for her," he said.

Two other clients made the finals at the Steamboat Springs Derby & Classic.

So much for the slump.

"I feel like my career is just now getting kicked off – finally," said Watts, who was born in 1961. "I'm riding some of the best horses of my career."

< 2 3 4 >

But he isn't quick to forget the long road to the top of his little hill. He's had his share of disappointments.

"I've had a lot of low moments, but I just tried not to let it get me down too far," he said. "The hardest thing is just keeping your head up and lose the pride because it will be your day to win again. We all can't win all the time. We just have to take it with a smile and keep going. I'm the one that chose this profession, it wasn't chosen for me. There are a lot of hills to cross before you get on flat ground. But that's what keeps it interesting."

After all, he noted, the horses are athletes, not machines. "They have their good days and their bad days," he said.

Watts' own bloodline may be as impressive as the cutters he trains. Two of the greatest influences on his professional and personal life include names widely respected in cutting circles – his father, James "Bubba" Watts and his uncle, the late Wayne Pooley.

"My dad kept me in good horses all my life," Watts said, describing his father (now retired) as "probably one of the best cowmen in the country."

Pooley's training fame includes the likes of Docs Hickory as well as Little Peppy, (sold to King Ranch) which he said became the all-time leading sire of National Cutting Horse Association competition cutting horses.

Watts left his hometown of Pleasanton, Texas, in 1979, when he graduated from high school. He competed on the rodeo team in college, but left university life for hands-on training. Though he picked up a little grooming from each of his trainer bosses, the biggest lessons came from his dad and uncle.

"MY DAD KEPT ME IN GOOD HORSES ALL MY LIFE."

"My dad and Wayne really taught me patience," he said. "They told me, 'They're not going to send you the really good horses until you prove yourself.' And I've had to ride just about anything that had a pulse and a little bit of hair."

But after Watts proved he could train the "not-so-good horses" to show quality and win a little money, people began to notice. And the really good horses came rolling in.

He's been on his own since 1988, and now is raising his family

< 2 3 5 >

the same way he was raised.

"I've worked on ranches my whole life, from cattle ranches to horse ranches," he said. "It kept me off the streets…not that I ever wanted to get on them. But I was around good Christian people my whole life. We're really fortunate. The Lord's really blessed us to no end."

Horses are a family affair at the Watts house. During the summer months, he packs up the whole crew for his travels, which enables him to spend extra time with them and gives his family a chance to join in the competition.

"We're constantly on the road," he said, noting that he attends all the major age competitions, cuttings and quarter horse events.

While his daughter Lauren, born in 1985, prefers showing steers, hogs and sheep in Future Farmers of America events, Watts' wife and his stepson – Maison Zuber – both show in cutting events.

"He's a heck of a little showman himself," Watts said, noting that Maison (born in 1991) has ranked as high as 12th in the world standings of the Junior Youth Cutting.

> "I WAS AROUND GOOD CHRISTIAN PEOPLE MY WHOLE LIFE. THE LORD'S REALLY BLESSED US TO NO END."

Older son Jerritt Watts, born in 1982, also shows and even takes to the ring with dad in the team-roping gig.

"I've been roping forever," Watts said, and Jerritt's been roping off and on since 1990. In 1996, he got really serious about it."

The two have won "a little money" in their team efforts, but Jerritt ropes to earn a college scholarship.

With or without his family in tow, Watts is gone at least two weekends a month. He'll be gone from a week to a month at a time.

"What I like most about the traveling part in the summer months is spending quality time with my family," he said. "And when they don't get to go with me, it's nice to drive through that gate and be home."

When he's not on the road, Watts' typical day starts at 5 a.m. to 6 a.m. His ranch hand helps feed and clean the stalls, while his boys help round up the day's work. They work as many horses as they can by lunchtime.

< 2 3 6 >

"It may be five horses or as many as 15, depending on the day," he said. "We don't try to work quantity, we try to give each horse the quality of time for what they need."

In the afternoon, they saddle up the 2-year olds, and then in the late evening finish up with the 3-year olds up to the show horses.

The next day they'll reverse the order of the horses. If it's breeding season, they breed the mares first thing in the morning and then get back to riding. There also is the occasional fence-mending project or loading horses for a trip to the vet. And Watts gives some morning and evening lessons with non-pros and amateurs.

"It's kind of like an assembly line out here," he said. "Everyone has their chores and pretty much knows what's going to happen the next day."

Watts starts training colts as 2-year olds, though, depending on size, he may begin breaking them the November of their yearling year. It takes about 90 days of riding and breaking before he'll put them on a cow.

> "IT'S KIND OF LIKE AN ASSEMBLY LINE OUT HERE. EVERYONE PRETTY MUCH KNOWS WHAT'S GOING TO HAPPEN THE NEXT DAY."

"Once they get pretty flexible, pretty supple, then I'll start them on a cow," he said. "I'll just put one cow in the arena and go around and around and around."

It takes at least a year to train, depending on the colt. By December of their third year, they're ready for the big event – the NCHA Futurity.

"But we don't try to make the big futurity on all our colts," he said, noting that he just grooms the ones with the most potential. The others compete in smaller futurities.

As for his training style, Watts says his emphasis is just on "letting them be a cow horse and getting them to stop hard."

When he's evaluating a horse, he starts with the bloodline "to give me a reason to look at them." In addition to good blood, he prefers a real low-hocked horse, a short back, a short neck and great confirmation.

"And everybody loves a pretty head," he said. "But like the old-timers say, you don't ride the head."

< 2 3 7 >

Watts admits that with experience his training style has changed a bit through the years.

"My horses a long time ago used to be pretty stiff," he said. "My horses are snappier now. They're not hesitant."

Watts is most proud of his stop. But he had to change his horses' style to get to that hard stop, which meant tweaking his training. That's when he learned just to let the horse be a cow horse.

"You can kind of rock' n' roll on them now, and that's the fun of showing," he said. "They just seem to be a little grittier. But you can't put that in all of them, because that may not be their style."

> "YOU CAN KIND OF ROCK' N' ROLL ON THEM NOW, AND THAT'S THE FUN OF SHOWING."

But living the horse life is definitely Watts' style. That rush of competition is second only to his family and faith.

"I thrive on competition," he said. "I thrive on that kind of pressure. I've always liked to show off for two and a half minutes, and then I'd humble myself after that bell rang."

Modesty seems to be a strong suit.

"I always said I never had a lot of skill or talent, but a lot of desire," Watts said. "I've developed some patience and put it in the Lord's hands."

< 2 3 8 >